Sociolinguistics

Bernard Spolsky is Professor of English
at Bar-Ilan University, Israel.

Oxford Introductions to Language Study

Series Editor H.G. Widdowson

Sociolinguistics

Bernard Spolsky

OXFORD UNIVERSITY PRESS

OXFORD

UNIVERSITY PRESS

Great Clarendon Street, Oxford OX2 6DP

Oxford University Press is a department of the University of Oxford.
It furthers the University's objective of excellence in research, scholarship,
and education by publishing worldwide in

Oxford New York

Auckland Cape Town Dar es Salaam Hong Kong Karachi
Kuala Lumpur Madrid Melbourne Mexico City Nairobi
New Delhi Shanghai Taipei Toronto

With offices in

Argentina Austria Brazil Chile Czech Republic France Greece
Guatemala Hungary Italy Japan Poland Portugal Singapore
South Korea Switzerland Thailand Turkey Ukraine Vietnam

OXFORD and OXFORD ENGLISH are registered trade marks of
Oxford University Press in the UK and in certain other countries

© Oxford University Press 1998

The moral rights of the author have been asserted

Database right Oxford University Press (maker)

First published 1998

2018

20 19

ISBN : 978 0 19 437211 4

Typeset by Wyvern 21 Ltd., Bristol, UK

Printed in China

for Elisheva and Yonatan

Contents

Preface

Purpose

What justification might there be for a series of introductions to language study? After all, linguistics is already well served with introductory texts: expositions and explanations which are comprehensive, authoritative, and excellent in their way. Generally speaking, however, their way is the essentially academic one of providing a detailed initiation into the discipline of linguistics, and they tend to be lengthy and technical: appropriately so, given their purpose. But they can be quite daunting to the novice. There is also a need for a more general and gradual introduction to language: transitional texts which will ease people into an understanding of complex ideas. This series of introductions is designed to serve this need.

Their purpose, therefore, is not to supplant but to support the more academically oriented introductions to linguistics: to prepare the conceptual ground. They are based on the belief that it is an advantage to have a broad map of the terrain sketched out before one considers its more specific features on a smaller scale, a general context in reference to which the detail makes sense. It is sometimes the case that students are introduced to detail without it being made clear what it is a detail *of*. Clearly, a general understanding of ideas is not sufficient: there needs to be closer scrutiny. But equally, close scrutiny can be myopic and meaningless unless it is related to the larger view. Indeed it can be said that the precondition of more particular enquiry is an awareness of what, in general, the particulars are about. This series is designed to provide this large-scale view of different areas of language study. As such it can serve as preliminary to (and precondition for) the more specific and specialized enquiry which students of linguistics are required to undertake.

But the series is not only intended to be helpful to such students. There are many people who take an interest in language without being academically engaged in linguistics *per se*. Such people may recognize the importance of understanding language for their own lines of enquiry, or for their own practical purposes, or quite simply for making them aware of something which figures so centrally in their everyday lives. If linguistics has revealing and relevant things to say about language, this should presumably not be a privileged revelation, but one accessible to people other than linguists. These books have been so designed as to accommodate these broader interests too: they are meant to be introductions to language more generally as well as to linguistics as a discipline.

Design

The books in the series are all cut to the same basic pattern. There are four parts: Survey, Readings, References, and Glossary.

Survey

This is a summary overview of the main features of the area of language study concerned: its scope and principles of enquiry, its basic concerns and key concepts. These are expressed and explained in ways which are intended to make them as accessible as possible to people who have no prior knowledge or expertise in the subject. The Survey is written to be readable and is uncluttered by the customary scholarly references. In this sense, it is simple. But it is not simplistic. Lack of specialist expertise does not imply an inability to understand or evaluate ideas. Ignorance means lack of knowledge, not lack of intelligence. The Survey, therefore, is meant to be challenging. It draws a map of the subject area in such a way as to stimulate thought and to invite a critical participation in the exploration of ideas. This kind of conceptual cartography has its dangers of course: the selection of what is significant, and the manner of its representation, will not be to the liking of everybody, particularly not, perhaps, to some of those inside the discipline. But these surveys are written in the belief that there must be an alternative to a technical account on the one hand and an idiot's guide on the other if linguistics is to be made relevant to people in the wider world.

Readings

Some people will be content to read, and perhaps re-read, the summary Survey. Others will want to pursue the subject and so will use the Survey as the preliminary for more detailed study. The Readings provide the necessary transition. For here the reader is presented with texts extracted from the specialist literature. The purpose of these Readings is quite different from the Survey. It is to get readers to focus on the specifics of what is said and how it is said in these source texts. Questions are provided to further this purpose: they are designed to direct attention to points in each text, how they compare across texts, and how they deal with the issues discussed in the Survey. The idea is to give readers an initial familiarity with the more specialist idiom of the linguistics literature, where the issues might not be so readily accessible, and to encourage them into close critical reading.

References

One way of moving into more detailed study is through the Readings. Another is through the annotated References in the third section of each book. Here there is a selection of works (books and articles) for further reading. Accompanying comments indicate how these deal in more detail with the issues discussed in the different chapters of the Survey.

Glossary

Certain terms in the Survey appear in bold. These are terms used in a special or technical sense in the discipline. Their meanings are made clear in the discussion, but they are also explained in the Glossary at the end of each book. The Glossary is cross-referenced to the Survey, and therefore serves at the same time as an index. This enables readers to locate the term and what it signifies in the more general discussion, thereby, in effect, using the Survey as a summary work of reference.

Use

The series has been designed so as to be flexible in use. Each title is separate and self-contained, with only the basic format in common. The four sections of the format, as described here, can be drawn upon and combined in different ways, as required by the needs, or interests, of different readers. Some may be content with the Survey and the Glossary and may not want to follow up the suggested References. Some may not wish to venture into the Readings. Again, the Survey might be considered as appropriate preliminary reading for a course in applied linguistics or teacher education, and the Readings more appropriate for seminar discussion during the course. In short, the notion of an introduction will mean different things to different people, but in all cases the concern is to provide access to specialist knowledge and stimulate an awareness of its significance. The series as a whole has been designed to provide this access and promote this awareness in respect to different areas of language study.

H.G.WIDDOWSON

Author's Preface

The invitation to write this short book is another of the many debts I owe to Henry Widdowson who, over the years that we have known each other, has managed to challenge and stimulate me continually. The special challenge this time is to follow in admired footsteps, for there have been many earlier and more detailed introductions to sociolinguistics from which I myself have benefited.

My task, as Widdowson defines it, is to sketch out a conceptual map for the interested reader of the relations between language and society. This is, in some respects, bound to be a personal view. My own curiosity about sociolinguistics grew out of language teaching. As a young high-school teacher in a New Zealand town, my interest was piqued by the bilingualism of some of my Maori students. Why, I naïvely asked, did boys who spoke Maori at home write better English essays than those whose parents spoke to them in a limited version of English? This early interest in the educational effects of language variation was to continue to be encouraged. I was fortunate enough to have a spell living in Montreal, a city whose people and scholars have made pioneering endeavours in the realm of multilingualism. Later in my career, an invitation to teach at the University of New Mexico landed me in the midst of an area where students were demonstrating for the right to remain bilingual. More recently, living in Israel, I have come to learn and appreciate the complex patterns of language that make up this country and its surroundings.

My attention to language variation has often had a practical bent, because I have also been involved in studying language learning and language policy. In spite of this, the central question I continue to ask, and the one that this volume encourages readers to ask, pertains to the close intertwining between a language and the social context in which it is used. Language and society may not be peculiarly human—how else can one appreciate social amoebae or the honey bee?—but they are such fundamental human phenomena that they cry out for better understanding.

Muhammad Amara and Henry Widdowson read earlier drafts of this book and made many useful suggestions. In preparing it, I have benefited from the help of the staff of the English Language Teaching Division at Oxford University Press who have once again demonstrated the friendly efficiency that makes an author's life easy.

This book is dedicated to my grandchildren, busy studying sociolinguistics in their own way.

BERNARD SPOLSKY

Survey

1
The social study of language

The scope of enquiry

Sociolinguistics is the field that studies the relation between language and society, between the uses of language and the social structures in which the users of language live. It is a field of study that assumes that human society is made up of many related patterns and behaviours, some of which are linguistic.

One of the principal uses of language is to communicate meaning, but it is also used to establish and to maintain social relationships. Watch a mother with a young child. Most of their talk is devoted to nurturing the social bond between them. Listen to two friends talking. Much of their conversation functions to express and refine their mutual compact of companionship. When you meet strangers, the way they talk informs you about their social and geographical backgrounds, and the way *you* talk sends subtle or blatant signals about what you think of them. It is these aspects of language use that sociolinguists study.

In the thirty years or so that it has been recognized as a branch of the scientific study of language, sociolinguistics has grown into one of the most important of the 'hyphenated' fields of linguistics. This term distinguishes the core fields of historical and descriptive linguistics (phonology, morphology, and syntax) from the newer interdisciplinary fields like psycholinguistics, applied linguistics, neurolinguistics, and sociolinguistics or the sociology of language. Stranded at times between sociology (one of the field's putative parents) and linguistics (the other), the practitioners of sociolinguistics have so far avoided the rigorous bounds of a single theoretical model, or the identifying shelter of a single professional organization. They apply a plethora of methods to a multitude of subjects that all have in common one single thread: languages and their use in social contexts.

There are indeed some sociolinguists who wonder how language can be studied in any other way. They believe that the search of the formal linguists like Noam Chomsky for an autonomous linguistics, with the goal of describing the idealized competence of an idealized monolingual in an idealized mono-variety speech community, is as doomed to failure as was the earlier effort of structural linguists to account for language structure without taking meaning into account.

While Noam Chomsky revolutionized many aspects of linguistics, he followed structural linguists like Leonard Bloomfield in choosing to study language autonomously, as a self-sufficient system. He aimed to find a basic universal grammatical structure that could account for the similarities in the organization of languages, without needing to appeal to the social context in which language is used. For Chomsky, the existence of variation in language simply confuses, diverting the linguist's attention from the wonderful abstract system that separates human language from other communication systems. For the sociolinguist, however, the most important verity is that a language—any language—is full of systematic variation, variation that can only be accounted for by appealing, outside language, to socially relevant forces and facts.

Sociolinguistics takes as its primary task to map linguistic variation on to social conditions. This mapping helps understand not just **synchronic variation** (variation at a single point of time), but also **diachronic variation** (variation over time) or language change.

The close intertwining of linguistic and social facts is crucial to a sociolinguistic approach. Even before small children can speak clearly, they develop a distinct style of address to be used when speaking to anyone or anything smaller. As they grow, they add more and more variations to their speech, and these come to be associated with recognizable **styles**. As early as the age of five, children asked to play roles try to imitate the styles of speech of many different people. These small variations in language that everyone acquires in normal upbringing can be used to identify us, or the person we are talking to, or the subject we are talking about. There is no single-style or single-variety speaker; no speech community that does not have a choice of varieties; and many fewer monolinguals than English speakers might imagine.

The existence of patterned variation in language makes it possible to identify ourselves and others as belonging to certain groups. The social prestige or stigma associated with these variations makes language a source of social and political power. Only by including both linguistic and social factors in our analysis can this complex but rule-governed behaviour be accounted for. To do this is the chosen goal of the sociolinguist.

Complementary approaches

Eschewing the normal acrimony of academic debate, we might say that the various complementary approaches to the study of language each find a different aspect of the complex phenomenon to be of enthralling interest. The formal linguist pursues an autonomous universal system, significant elements of which are to be explained by the very design and structure of the human brain. The psycholinguist asks how such a system works and how it can be learned or lost. The sociolinguist asks how it is used in a living and complex speech community. The answers to each of these questions is important to the applied linguist, concerned, among other matters, with how to help people learn language and how to use it effectively to deal with problems of practical everyday life.

Just as the formal linguist and the psycholinguist focus their attention on the language as a system with universal features, so the sociolinguist looks at the complex connections between the variations within a language and the matching variations in the social groups that use it. Why, the song asks, do *I* say /təmˈɑːtəʊ/ and *you* say /təmˈeɪtəʊ/. Why do I say 'Good morning!' to some people, and 'Hi!' to others? How did Professor Higgins know which parts of Eliza Doolittle's speech needed to be changed to make her pass for a member of the upper class? Sociolinguistics is all about variation, and seeks socially relevant explanations for regular patterns of variation in language use.

A sociolinguist is interested in the way that members of a speech community can, and do, identify and respond to fine differences in language usage that are associated, within a speech community, with social or economic or political or religious or cultural or other divisions of the society. At what is often called the **micro** end of sociolinguistics, the sociolinguist's goal might be to show how specific differences in pronunciation or grammar lead members of a speech community to make judgments about the education or economic status of a speaker. In New York City, for instance, pronouncing the word 'this' as /dɪs/ or pronouncing 'bird' as /bɔɪd/, marks the social class of the speaker. In the same way, the choice of lexical items (saying 'doctor's surgery' instead of 'doctor's office') makes clear on which side of the Atlantic a speaker of English has been living. Over-average use of tag questions would seem to mark young females in New Zealand. A high proportion of words from Modern Standard Arabic marks the vernacular speech of educated Arabs. As much as speech itself communicates content, so the form of speech, the selection among available socially marked **variants**, communicates important social information about the speaker and the listener and about their relationship to each other. In other words, adapting Marshall McLuhan's famous words, the medium (the variety chosen) becomes the message itself.

At the other—the **macro**—end of the spectrum, sometimes labelled the **sociology of language** as distinct from sociolinguistics, the scholar's primary attention turns from the specific linguistic phenomena to the whole of a language or **variety** (a term we use to include any identifiable kind of language). In macro-sociolinguistics, we treat language (and a specific language) alongside other human cultural phenomena. We might ask, for instance, about the significance of a group of immigrants shifting completely to a new language or maintaining their old one for some purposes. Why did most immigrants to the USA from Northern Europe drop their home language so fast, while Asian immigrants to Britain seem to be keeping theirs alive? How did Welsh survive English occupation, or how did Basque and Catalan stay alive under Franco's policy of enforcing the use of Castilian Spanish? We might investigate the close bonds between language choice and social identity, asking why their language remained so important to Maoris, Basques, or Frisians that they have been willing to undertake political action to preserve it. We might ask why speakers of certain varieties are influential and powerful, and why speakers of other varieties are regularly discriminated against. These questions concern the use of a language or a language variety as a whole rather than individual variations, and asking them makes the study of language a means to understanding a society.

Some scholars use this difference of perspective to divide the field into two. They want to distinguish between sociolinguistics, which emphasizes the social influences on language, and the sociology of language, which emphasizes the role of language in society. In this book, however, I shall examine both aspects together, arguing for a common concern for the connection between language and society rather than a need to give priority to one or the other.

There are, as we will see, a large number of discrete but related phenomena that can be considered from the two perspectives. Included are topics like language and gender, social stratification, language planning, language and power, language and ethnicity, language and nationalism. To capture relevant dimensions of the patterns under study, the sociolinguist is regularly forced to broaden the scope of enquiry from the parent disciplines of linguistics and sociology to other fields like social psychology, gender studies, public policy management, political science, and history.

If there is a common theme that emerges from the studies of sociolinguists, it is that the complex interplay of language structure with social structure means that any user of language is constantly responding to and signalling social information. My identity (or rather my various identities) is recognizable from my choice among all the variants that a language offers. One might even go so far as to claim that it is this choice of identity that accounts, better than the other factors we will consider, for the observable variation in natural speech.

But before we can consider these more specific topics and the theories held to explain them, it is valuable to make clear what the data of sociolinguistics are, and what methods are used to collect these data.

The methods of enquiry

What to study and *how* to study it are closely related questions. A theory tells us which facts count as data. A science advances either by posing new important questions about the data or by finding new ways of observing data to answer important questions. Noam Chomsky initiated a revolution in linguistics by asking how to account for the fact that everyone who learns a language (a first language, that is to say) shows evidence of control of rules that are not evident from normal exposure to people speaking. Sociolinguists ask a different question: how to account for the variation that exists in every language. Because of what they study, they are just as concerned with how to answer the question as with the question itself.

The reason for this concern is because we need to observe a dynamic phenomenon in its natural setting. In biology, one common way of studying frogs is by dissecting them, but of course a dead frog doesn't do very much. In sociolinguistics, the analogous riddle is what Labov labelled the **observer's paradox**, namely: how can we observe the way people speak when they are not being observed?

The enigma arises because sociolinguists believe that language use is always sensitive to the social relations among the participants in a speech event. We speak differently to superiors, to colleagues, to friends, and to children. Our speech patterns regularly change when another person (especially a stranger) enters the conversation. Even young children quickly develop markedly different styles for talking to different people. Given this sensitivity of speech to audience, how can a linguist, who is a stranger and an outside observer, witness and record the **vernacular** and unmonitored speech patterns that close friends use among themselves? Doesn't the presence of the sociolinguist kill the naturalness of the speech just as effectively as the dissector's scalpel kills the frog? There has been no definitive answer. Sociolinguists have countered the paradox in different ways, as we shall see.

What are the data?

The question of what constitutes interpretable data is a key one in any discipline. In sociolinguistics, there is a tension between the observers and the quantifiers. Joshua Fishman has recounted that when he and John Gumperz were working together on a study of bilingualism among Puerto Ricans in the Jersey City *barrio*, Gumperz would occasionally ask him to produce evidence to back up an assertion. Fishman, with his background in sociology and psychology, would bring in bundles of computer print-out of statistical calculations. When Gumperz himself was similarly challenged by Fishman, Gumperz, trained as an ethnographer, would describe a conversation he had overheard at a party the night before. Note that Fishman used elicited data that could be analysed statistically, while Gumperz discovered his data through observation of the use of language in a natural setting.

If we try to understand the basis for these two approaches, we might say that sociologists seek their evidence in the patterns underlying the answers of a large number of people to many carefully designed questions. The social forces that control individual speech behaviour are expressed, sociologists believe, in the statistically determinable tendencies that can be extracted by analysing large quantities of data. Ethnographers, on the other hand, trained to compare the behaviour of individuals in one culture with the patterns of behaviour observed in many other cultures, have learned to present their intuitions through the interpretation of single events that they carefully observe. The two approaches are complementary.

Whatever method they choose, what sociolinguists are looking for is evidence of socially accepted rules accounting for variations in speech. The evidence is in part the speech variation (the differences in pronunciation or word choice, or in grammatical choice), in part the characteristics of the speaker (age, gender, education, place of birth, and domicile), and in part the nature of the speech encounter (its place, its topic, the role relations of the speakers). Some of these data can be collected by observation, some by elicitation. Whether to trust the observation is of course a problem: the speaker might be pretending or lying, the observer might be looking too hard or not noticing something critical. All of these methodological problems are inevitable in the study of a living phenomenon like language in its social use.

Given these concerns, many studies make use of multiple data collected in a number of different ways. If the observed encounter shows the same pattern as the carefully analysed sample of speech, and if the attitudinal questionnaire is consistent with the statistical observations, a sociolinguist can be more confident that the account of the underlying structure is valid.

The sociolinguist at work

In practice, a number of workable solutions have been found to the 'observer's paradox' of collecting natural speech samples. To analyse variation in pronunciation, sociolinguists studying microlinguistic variation regularly count the frequency of occurrence of a linguistic feature under defined social conditions. For finer differences, they may make precise instrumental measurements of significant speech sounds. In order to obtain the samples for this analysis, natural speech must be recorded on tape. This produces the methodological problem. Won't speakers become self-conscious, and try to make their speech clearer or more standard in the presence of a tape-recorder? Are the data collected in this way natural?

Clandestine recording has been tried and largely abandoned. There are practical reasons, for the tapes are usually noisy and require very expensive processing. There are also ethical ones. Fifty years ago, a study of spoken English could be based on surreptitiously recorded telephone conversations passing through a university switchboard. In a climate of greater respect for the privacy of their sources, sociolinguists now ask their subjects for permission to use the tapes that they have made. Tape-recorders are now in the open, and researchers are generally satisfied that any initial anxiety effecting the level of formality will disappear as an interview continues.

The **sociolinguistic interview**, modelled on the format developed by William Labov for his now classic doctoral study of New York City English, is one of the most common techniques for gathering samples of language. In the interview, the sociolinguist talks to the subject, attempting to elicit examples of various kinds of speech. The normal stylistic level for an interview like this is fairly formal, for the two people speaking are strangers. There are ways to modify the level of formality. The easiest alteration is in the direction of more careful attention to speech, by giving the person being interviewed a passage or a list of words to read. It is more difficult to relax the formality. Occasional bursts of informal speech occur when a speaker switches to a topic outside the interview, such as when a mother being interviewed by a sociolinguist speaks to her child who has come into the room. Another circumstance is when the speaker is emotionally involved in an event he or she is narrating. Taking advantage of this, an interviewer might ask a question about an occasion when the speaker's life was in danger and so obtain less self-conscious speech.

Interviews provide a good deal of data, and are therefore invaluable in studying in depth the language variation of the subjects. By selecting a sample of subjects carefully, the researcher can make sure that significant social types (for example, by gender, age, education, occupation) are represented. One way to do this is to draw the subjects from a sample previously studied in a sociological survey. But interviews are expensive in time and effort, so that the number of different people studied is limited.

For studying larger populations, one technique is the covert collection of **non-intrusive responses**. Labov used this technique when he asked salespeople in three New York department stores a question to which the answer was 'Fourth floor'. This utterance gave him two post-vocalic 'r's and a 'th' to record. By asking for a repetition, he obtained a second set of data, this time with added stress. A related approach has been tried using telephone calls made in different languages in a multilingual city, to find out whether there was prejudice against speakers of one of the languages.

Once a natural speech sample has been collected, it must be analysed. Usually, the linguist chooses a **variable**, a specific feature that previous observation suggests is likely to prove of social significance. In New York English, the pronunciation of /r/ after a vowel is such a feature, and in Palestinian vernacular Arabic it is the use of /tʃ/ rather than /k/ in the word for dog, *kalb* or *chalb*. Each occasion where the feature could occur is counted, and the percentage of each **variant** under specific conditions (for example, by speaker or by style) provides statistical data which can be compared with other factors.

Because the interviewer usually has some clear preconceptions about what phenomena are likely to be interesting, a sociolinguistic interview follows a prepared protocol. After an opening general conversation, there are likely to be questions about children's games and rhymes to elicit older vernacular usage, and a question about some momentous event that might encourage the subject to talk unself-consciously. There may also be word lists to read or pictures to name to check out more careful pronunciation of selected sounds or to check out variations in names of objects. An interview provides extensive statistical data on a large number of linguistic variations.

For sociolinguists working in the ethnographic tradition, the main technique is the recording (either at the same time with a tape-recorder or more usually on paper immediately after the event) of natural speech events in which they have participated. As in other **ethnographic observation**, observers' previous experiences have prepared them to recognize significant exchanges. These examples are not always open to statistical analysis, but are usually vivid cases which encourage our acceptance of the validity of the ethnographer's authority and his or her assertion that they represent a general rule and not an aberrant case.

To obtain statistically analysable data about attitudes and behaviours, a common technique is the questionnaire, a prepared list of questions to which strangers are asked to respond. Questionnaires have been used mainly by social psychologists, who ask the people they are studying (or a carefully selected group of them who can be shown to represent the wider population) a set of questions about themselves, their beliefs, and their behaviours. By repeating the same question in different forms, the psychologist can get some idea of the reliability of the answers, and by careful wording of questions, attention can be focused on those features that are to be analysed. One of the difficulties with direct questionnaires is that they focus attention on the issue so clearly that people answering might tell you what they think you want to know. Another difficulty is that questionnaires are fixed in advance and so they might leave out questions that seem interesting later on. In this respect, interviews are much more flexible, but of course limited because of the time they take to give and analyse.

Questionnaires are particularly useful in gathering demographic data ('How old are you?' 'How many years did you spend at school?' 'What is your occupation?'). They are also used to study attitudes ('What language do you think is the most useful?' 'What language is the most beautiful?'). With *can-do* questions, they are used to obtain self-reports on language proficiency ('What languages can you read?' 'In what languages can you carry on a conversation?').

The approach in this book

This chapter started out by defining the field of sociolinguistics, and setting as its concern the relationship between language and society. The field of study is focused on variations in language that may be shown to be closely related to variations in society. We then considered the methodological issues that continue to dominate discussion of the field.

In Chapter 2 an approach to language study is introduced derived from anthropology called the ethnography of speaking or communication. This approach, which starts with language in use rather than with its abstract structure, will provide us with a basis for the study of conversation and of politeness. The way that language variation can be located geographically and socially will start to be explored in Chapter 3. The division into speech communities, and the geographical and political factors that lead to the division of languages into identifiable dialects, are also described in that chapter. Social factors are turned to in Chapter 4. After defining the notion of style to represent the socially determined variation in the speech of an individual, gender and social-class effects on language are examined. In Chapter 5 there is a discussion on the bilingual—the speaker with two distinct languages—and bilingualism—the effects of this knowledge and the ways that the bilingual decides which language to use. In Chapter 6 bilingualism is viewed as a phenomenon from a social perspective, considering the nature of multilingual societies, the forces leading to shifts in language use, and the establishment of stable bilingualism or diglossia. In Chapter 7 ways in which the knowledge gained by sociolinguistics is applied to social problems are discussed, such as language policy and planning and language education.

2

The ethnography of speaking and the structure of conversation

The ethnography of speaking

Sociolinguists believe that the study of language must go beyond the sentences that are the principal focus of descriptive and theoretical linguistics. It must go beyond language and bring in social context. It must deal with the 'real' texts that make up human communication and the social situations in which they are used. The focus of attention shifts from the sentence to the act of communication, the **speech event**.

Building on a model of communication first proposed by Roman Jakobson, Dell Hymes suggested that any communicative use of language or speech event is constituted by seven distinct factors, each associated with a different function. The first two are the speaker-writer and the hearer-reader; the third is the message form passed between them which is drawn from the resources of a speech code. The message form expresses a topic, some propositional content which is passed by some physical means, some channel, visual in the case of writing or sign language or aural in the case of speech. The speech event is located in some setting or other. It is possible to study these one at a time, but each must be included to understand the working of the system. In particular cases, one or more of these factors can be emphasized. The emotive or expressive function stresses the speaker-writer's attitude. The referential or denotative function stresses the topic. Some messages just check that the channel is open ('Can you hear me?') or assure that it is ('Uh huh').

Dell Hymes proposed that this model should provide the basis for an **ethnography of speaking** (sometimes also called an ethnography of communication), which is an approach to the description of speech events that calls for an analysis of each of the relevant factors. Each of them may be studied independently, but all are closely interrelated in forming the structure of the whole event. For each **genre** or kind of speech event, the factors are realized and related in appropriate ways.

Consider for instance how we might describe a sermon. The typical speaker is a clergyman, the listeners a group of people constituting a religious congregation, the setting a church or synagogue or mosque, the channel direct voice or voice amplified by loudspeaker (or in a modified version, transmitted by radio or television), the message form (i.e. the actual sounds, words, and sentences uttered by the speaker) a register of a language presumably understood by the congregation, and the topic some appropriate religious content.

Underlying the event is a complex set of socially recognized rules, which can be most easily recognized by considering possible breaches of them. Imagine for instance a preacher who stands there and says nothing, or reads out an account of a football match. Or think what might happen when the preacher uses for his sermon a liturgical language like Latin or Coptic or Sanskrit that is still used for prayer but that the congregation may no longer understand. Or a congregation that sings a hymn while the preacher is speaking, or goes to sleep. Or when a lecturer starts to give a sermon on morality in a physics class. These breaches of normal conditions for a sermon suggest how one might build a set of rules to describe a typical sermon as a speech event. One might do the same for other recognizable speech events, like a chemistry lecture, or a dinner-party conversation, or a bargaining session, or a lovers' quarrel.

The major value of the ethnography of speaking to sociolinguistics was in setting up an approach to language that went far beyond the attempt to account for single written or spoken sentences. It widened the scope to include all aspects of the speech event. This proves invaluable in considering the structure of one of the commonest of speech events, the conversation, when two or more people speak to each other.

The structure of conversations

Linguists have as a general rule focused on the smaller units of language like sounds, words, and sentences, leaving it to other scholars to examine the larger units that make up speech events. In the case of the written language, the study of texts and genres has been the task of the literary scholar. There is also a crossover field of stylistics and poetics where occasionally linguists and literary scholars study the same objects, and more occasionally talk to each other about their different views. Oral literary texts were also studied by folklorists and literary scholars, but the study of natural chunks of spoken language was generally ignored by linguists until ethnographers, sociologists, and sociolinguists started to explore its structure.

Because so much earlier linguistic analysis was based on the written language, it is understandable that the sentence should have been considered as the important unit to study. But sentences are less useful in the study of speech, for if you look at the verbatim transcription of a normal conversation, you will see how few sentences are finished. More usefully, the **conversational interchange** is the basic unit of the spoken language. Its structure was first teased out in some innovative studies of telephone conversations, where it was shown that a normal telephone conversation has a number of distinct parts:

Who	Utterance	Comment
Caller	(dials; phone rings)	This is the *summons*
Other	Hello?	*Answer*
Caller	Hello, this is Joe. Is that Bill?	*Identification*
Other	Yes	*Identity stage*
Caller	The meeting is still on?	*Message*
Other	Yes. I'll see you there.	*Acknowledgement*
Caller	OK. Bye.	*Close*
Caller		*Hangs up*

How do we know that telephone conversations are rule-governed behaviour? One quick way is to imagine what is likely to happen if someone doesn't follow one of the rules we propose. If when you make a telephone call, you hear the receiver being lifted but no one speaks, the conversation is usually stuck. You will usually issue another summons, saying something like 'Hello! Are you there?' If, on the other hand, like many children who have not learned the rules yet, you start speaking as soon as the receiver is lifted, not waiting for the answerer to say something, there is a moment of confusion. If you call a number and hear a voice saying 'I'm busy at the moment. Please call back' or 'I'm not here at the moment. Please leave a message after the beep', you assume you are talking to a machine and behave accordingly. To hang up without a formal close is considered abrupt and insulting behaviour.

There is a great deal of culturally and socially determined variation in the possible choices within the pattern set out here. In England, people commonly answer the phone by reciting their telephone number. Telephone operators in offices are trained to answer by identifying their employer: 'English Department. Good morning!' Intercom calls are answered with 'Yes' rather than 'Hello'. Asking 'Is X there?' is interpreted as asking to speak to X. There are national differences in these rules. In some countries, it is considered impolite to ask to speak to someone else before initiating a series of polite social interchanges with the person answering. The development of answering machines and of voice-mail is adding new structures to the rules, setting new challenges for the novice or the conservative.

The important notion from our point of view is that there is a formal structure to conversations, in part determined by the nature of the event (until the answerer says something, the caller has no one to talk to), and in part determined by social rules (what it is appropriate to say to specific people in defined circumstances).

This quick analysis of the telephone conversation demonstrates the existence of socially structured rules for conversational interchanges. There have been studies of various aspects of conversation, such as the nature of **service encounters** (such as between a customer and a seller), the rules for turn-taking and interruption, the organization of invitations, and the normal patterns of social intercourse in casual conversations.

Service encounters also have a fairly straightforward underlying structure. The first element is similar to the bell ringing in a telephone conversation: engaging the attention of the person meant to give the service. The task here is to establish the channel between speaker and hearer. This varies according to the social situation and cultural pattern. In some cultures and situations, it leads to a preliminary social exchange; in others, it involves simply catching the eye of the clerk or ticket-seller and making a gesture without saying anything. Shop-keepers in the Middle East remark on the brusqueness of tourists who start their conversation by pointing to something and saying 'How much?' Their normal conversational interchanges starts with a formal set of greeting, including enquiries after the health of the parties and their presumed families, comments on the weather or some other neutral subject, and finally a mention that there is some commercial purpose to the event. In other words, they require that the topic be broached only after a social exchange.

One kind of service encounter that has been highly developed in some societies is the process of bargaining, where the two parties seek to arrive at a price that satisfies both. In Middle Eastern usage, this often involves appeals to a neutral bystander, who initially is expected to agree with the buyer that the first price is too high, but is ultimately expected to confirm that the seller's last price is a fair one. This kind of negotiation is even more highly developed in industrial bargaining and in diplomatic exchanges.

Turn-taking, the question of who speaks, is one of the most intriguing aspects of conversational interchange. The physical constraint is obvious. If two people are speaking at once, they and others find it difficult to understand everything said. In various formal situations, there are clear rules on the order of speaking. In a classroom, teachers claim the right to control turn-taking. The teacher speaks more or less when he or she wants, and grants permission to students to talk. In a parliament or other public meeting, a chairperson is given the authority to determine who can speak and for how long. In trials, there are clear rules on who speaks first, who has the last word, who may ask questions, and who must answer them. Lay witnesses are often confused and usually at a disadvantage in their lack of understanding of these rules.

In informal conversations and informal meetings, the issue of turn-taking is often quite complex, depending on power and status. Who has the **floor** (the right to talk at any given moment) varies according to rules of the social group. Once someone has the floor, it is possible to try to interrupt, but a speaker can ignore this. Silence sometimes leaves the floor open, but there are **turn-holders**—ways of signalling that the speaker intends to continue after a break—like 'umm ...' or avoidance of a final intonation pattern.

Much of the study of discourse has been carried out with a focus on the meaning or topic rather than the other more social factors, and is therefore better considered under the rubric of pragmatics. Here, our focus is the social, and we will analyse in some detail two matters concerning the influence of social aspects of the relation of the speaker-writer and the listener-reader in the limitations set in choice of the message form. First we ask, what is politeness and how does it control speech? Second, we will look at the socially controlled choice of forms involved in selecting an appropriate term with which to address the person to whom you are talking.

Politeness and politeness formulas

Because speech events regularly include both a speaker-writer and a listener-reader, it is not surprising that language is particularly sensitive, in the rules for speech use, to the relations between the two parties. Just as a good actor can utter a single sentence expressing a wide range of emotional states of the speaker, so the choice of an appropriate message form can be modified to express a wide range of attitudes of the speaker to the listener. Given the same general situation, I can pass information or make a request or simply greet in a whole set of different ways that will define my attitude to the listener and the importance I give him or her.

In its simplest terms, **politeness** consists of this recognition of the listener and his or her rights in the situation. Requests, which are an imposition on the listener, are mitigated by being made indirectly, as questions ('Could you possibly pass me the salt?') or as statements ('I think that is the salt beside your plate'), or by adding formulas like 'Please' and 'if you would be so kind'. Social relations are eased by complimenting ('I do like your new car!' or 'Congratulations'). In some languages, there are elaborated sets of politeness formulas, like in Arabic saying *mabruk* to someone who has just bought something new, or *naʔiman* to someone who has just had a haircut or a bath or a short nap. For each formula, there is an appropriate reply, *'allah ybarik fik* (may God bless you) to the first and *'allah ynʔam ʔalek* (may God refresh you) to the second. In American English, the equivalent is saying 'You're welcome' in reply to 'Thank you'.

The most common kinds of politeness formulas are involved with greetings. Greetings are the basic oil of social relations. To fail to greet someone who expects to be greeted signals either some unusual distraction or a desire to insult the person. Each social group has its own set of rules about who should be greeted, who should greet first, and what is an appropriate form of greeting.

English greetings range from an informal 'Hi!' through a neutral 'Good morning' to a slowly disappearing formal 'How do you do!' It is common to add a second part of the greeting, a purely phatic 'How are you!' to which no reply is expected. Arab greetings use an elaborate set of paired greetings-plus-responses, depending on time of day or other social aspects of the situation.

The study of greetings, therefore, provides a first useful method of exploring the structure of a social group. A second area showing patterned variation in speech and similarly studied within the ethnography of communication has been the conditions on the use of terms of address.

Terms of address

The choice of second-person pronoun and the related phenomenon of **terms of address** in Western European languages in particular shows the formalization of politeness and status in a language. A number of languages offer the same sort of choice as French of addressing a single person using either the singular pronoun *tu* or the plural *vous*.

In earlier usage, the plural V form (*vous* in French, *Sie* in

German) was used to address someone of higher status, who would return the T form (*tu* in French, *du* in German). Thus, a servant would use V to a master who would reply with T. In medieval French, this moved through the whole chain of being, with God speaking to the angels as T, or men using T for animals. V could also be used between equals. There developed over time a tendency to switch from V–V use to T–T use, as a sign of intimacy. The French verb *tutoyer*, to use T to someone, refers to this change of familiarity. At one stage, in German student society before the First World War, the switch was accompanied by a formal ceremony. In early twentieth-century French society, two adult males who had served in the army together would use T to each other. While the pattern has been relaxed, it remains impolite to use T to a stranger. There have been complaints that students in Canadian-French immersion programmes are sometimes addressed only with the T form, and so have not learned the appropriate use of the V form with adult strangers.

With the growing egalitarianism of modern life, there has been a slow breakdown in the formality of address systems. The ideologically based switch from V to T associated with communism has been documented in Russian novels of the period. French children return T to their parents. Many speakers of Swedish now use T even to strangers.

A related phenomenon in languages that do not have the T/V distinction is the use of address terms. English once had the *thou/you* distinction and still offers a range of address terms, ranging from Title Alone (Sir, Your Majesty, Madam, Constable) through Title + Last Name (Mr Jones, Dr Smith, Lord Clark, Miss Jones, Mrs Jones, perhaps Ms Jones) to First Name to Multiple Names (including Nicknames). The conditions for choosing vary socially. Increasingly, in North American and British academic circles, people who have just been introduced as 'Professor X, meet Dr Y' move immediately to first names. There are still interesting cases of uneven usage. American doctors and dentists use first names to all their patients, but expect Dr X in return. Teachers in many societies receive Title or Title + Last Name, but return first name (or in some schools, last name).

In Arabic, there is an elaborate set of address patterns. One interesting feature is the custom of addressing friends and acquaintances by the name of their eldest son: a woman is addressed as *um Ahmed*, mother of Ahmed, and a man as *abu Ahmed*, father of Ahmed. The custom is even extended to people without children.

Title plus first or last name is a common pattern in many languages. Non-relatives may also be addressed with terms of relationships, as in an English pattern of training children to address adults of the parent's generation as Uncle John or Auntie Mary. In Tongan, on the other hand, while there is a complex hierarchical system with almost feudal ranks, people are never addressed by kinship or other titles, but only by their name.

Military usage related to address systems shows special patterns. Peace-time armies with strict discipline and emphasis on ceremonial are likely to have strict rules for addressing superiors. In the US Marine Corps, senior officers were addressed in the third person ('Would the General like me to bring him a cup of coffee?') and other officers received 'sir' from their inferiors. Non-commissioned officers were addressed by rank ('Yes, sergeant.') In a different setting, such as under battle conditions, things changed. An officer was addressed directly, often by a regular nickname. Company commanders, for instance, were addressed as 'Skipper' and sergeant-majors as 'Gunny'. More democratic armies often make a point of dropping special address rules along with saluting. These changes parallel the changes from V to T under similar circumstances.

The ethnography of speaking moved the focus of analysis from the sentence to the speech event, and offered a first approach to the analysis of natural speech, by showing patterns that could be understood if social information were included. In this, as in any other study of language in use, the aspect that became more obvious to the sociolinguist was the existence of regularly patterned variation. It provided a wider canvas on which to paint the complexity of language behaviour in its social setting, and a technique for capturing some of the ways in which each may reflect the other. It opened up the way to the study of language in use, to the importance of different channels, to the critical importance of relations between speaker and hearer, and to the social context of language.

Against this wider background, we return to the central issue with which sociolinguistics is concerned, the existence and nature of regularly patterned variation in language and the role of social factors in accounting for this regularity of pattern. In the ethnography of speaking, the setting is usually defined socially. But setting can also be defined in geographical terms, and can also be placed in terms of the patterning of social class.

3
Locating variation in speech

Speech communities and repertoires

The non-hyphenated fields of linguistics like phonology, semantics, and syntax focus on the language system ideally abstracted from all social context. Psycholinguistics deals with the individual speaker's acquisition and use of language, and relates this to mental processes. Sociolinguistics is concerned with language *in situ* and *in vivo*, alive in its geographical and social setting and space. What this space is like, we now consider. To start with, because our main interest is in social matters, we will deal with social space, and look for the location of varieties of speech within definable social units.

Some of the units with which we are concerned are already familiar and established social groupings. Thus, we can study the language of families, neighbourhoods, villages, cities, states, countries, or regions. However, for theory building and planning observation, we need a more flexible and abstract concept, provided by the notion of a speech community.

For general linguistics, a **speech community** is all the people who speak a single language (like English or French or Amharic) and so share notions of what is same or different in phonology or grammar. This would include any group of people, wherever they might be, and however remote might be the possibility of their ever wanting or being able to communicate with each other, all using the same language. The notion is preserved in such a concept as 'la francophonie', the French-speaking world, and it can serve as the basic slogan for political co-operation. Underlying it is the idea of a group of people who could, if they wanted, speak to each other.

Sociolinguists, however, find it generally more fruitful to focus on the language practices of a group of people who do in fact have the opportunity to interact and who, it often turns out, share not just a single language but a **repertoire** of languages or varieties. For the sociolinguist, the speech community is a complex interlocking network of communication whose members share knowledge about and attitudes towards the language use patterns of others as well as themselves. There is no theoretical limitation on the location and size of a speech community, which is in practice defined by its sharing a set of language varieties (its repertoire) and a set of norms for using them.

The idea that the members of a speech community share norms about the selection of varieties is important. Though they might not all know and use each of the varieties, they recognize the conditions under which other members of the community believe that it is appropriate to use each of them. Londoners recognize Cockney and Mayfair varieties of English though they may themselves use neither. A small social network (such as regular patrons of a coffee shop) forms a speech community, and so does a large metropolis or a country, a region, or a communication network (like the Internet). In each case, the goal of sociolinguistic study of such a community is to relate the significant language varieties to the significant social groups and situations.

In small Israeli Palestinian villages, there are commonly four significant varieties making up the linguistic repertoire: the village vernacular (a dialectal variant of Palestinian Arabic), Classical or Modern Standard Arabic (the *fus-Ha* taught in school and used for writing and public speaking), Modern Israeli Hebrew (learned by those who worked outside the village or went to high school), and some school-learned English. The village dialect is considered appropriate for most daily activities; Modern Standard Arabic is used only in educational or religious or formal public functions; Hebrew is kept for use outside the village; and English for educational use.

In a city, the pattern is likely to be even more complex. Inside the walls of the Old City of Jerusalem, there are thirty or more languages used by different residents in different settings. In Hong Kong, while most local Chinese use Cantonese most of the time, many have learned and use *Putonghoa* (Standard Mandarin), whose status changed with the reversion to Chinese sovereignty, and all who go to school learn and (less often) use English. In Toronto, Melbourne, New York, or London, English is the common language, but in certain neighbourhoods it is regularly found sharing the repertoire with dozens, even scores, of immigrant languages. In other cities, like Brussels, there is a clear division between areas where French or Flemish dialects are dominant.

The speech repertoire may be divided functionally as well as spatially. On the Navajo Reservation in the Western United States, most people *spoke* Navajo up to a few years ago, but most *writing* was done in English. The many FM radio stations announced the Country and Western music they played most of the time in Navajo, but the tribal newspaper was published only in English. The Tribal Council conducted its meetings in Navajo (using an interpreter for communication with government officials), but its decisions were recorded and published in English. Most schools at that time tried to teach Navajo-speaking pupils to read English. In the last few years, more and more children have been starting to speak English.

The notion of speech repertoire and community is also useful in looking at variation within a single language. In a Palestinian village that between 1949 and 1967 was arbitrarily divided in half, with half in Israel and half in the Jordanian West Bank, there is still evidence, twenty-five years after the division was ended, of the existence of two quite distinct varieties of spoken Arabic. Studies of Germany after reunification have shown signs of new linguistic differentiation between the Western and the Eastern half, something added to the older North–South dialectal variations. New York or London studied as speech communities show not just regional variation but also social variation.

Smaller **networks**—groups of people who communicate with each other regularly—also contain consistent patterns. One might, for instance, study the linguistic differences that make up the communicative repertoire in a modern office or research centre equipped with computers and telephones and faxes. A researcher with a problem might send off a quick e-mail question to a colleague in the next room, or ask the same question by telephone. If the answer is complicated, it might be handled by sending (by fax or computer) a copy of a previously written paper. When the exchanges become too involved, the colleagues might arrange (by phone or e-mail) a face-to-face meeting. Each of these communications media will involve different stylistic choices, and the variants can be considered as making up the repertoire. In the same way, international organizations might, like the European Community, have a formal policy governing choice of language from the repertoire available.

The speech community is, therefore, the abstract 'space' studied in sociolinguistics, the location in which the patterned variations in selection from the available repertoire takes place.

Dialect

There are longer-established approaches to the issue of variation as a result of geographical location. Well before sociolinguistics became identified as a discipline, students of language gave serious attention to the variations in language that correlated with the locality where the language was spoken. The study of regional **dialects** played a major role in the **historical linguistics** that flourished in the late eighteenth and the nineteenth centuries, until the interest in diachronic changes (over time) was challenged by the concern for synchronic description of a language system at any one time, with a preference for the present.

It was long obvious (and sometimes troubling) that people who spoke what they considered the same language had different words for the same thing or different pronunciations for the same word. The Bible has an account of the first exploitation of this difference. In the Book of Judges (12: 4–6), there is the story of a struggle between the Gileadites and the Ephraimites. After the battle, the Gileadites made use of the different pronunciation of the Ephraimites (who called a small river *sibboleth* rather than *shibboleth*) to identify the enemy. Two thousand years later, William Caxton, in the preface to one of the first English books that he printed, bemoaned the difficulty he had in choosing between northern and southern English forms. Should one print *eggys* or *eyren*, he asked, and how would a speaker of the northern dialect fare ordering eggs in London? Regional differences in variety continue to be the characteristic of humour (a southern accent is laughed at in Tunisia just as in the USA) and prejudice (it is not always easy to book a room in a northern US hotel by telephone if you have a Black or Southern accent).

The earliest scholars concerned with regional dialectal variation were the philologists who set out first to explain differences in manuscripts according to the place where the manuscript was written, and later used their collected observations to reconstruct the history of the language. Essentially, there are two principles underlying social accounts of dialect variation. The first is that all languages change over time, as new words are added to deal with new concepts or as contact with other languages and 'phonetic drift' leads to modifications in phonology. The second is that people who communicate with each other tend to speak similarly. Assume a group of people all setting off from one place where they lived together and spoke the same language, with sub-groups stopping off and forming communities isolated by distance or geographical boundaries from other speakers of the language. Over time, the language spoken in each place will change. The longer the groups are isolated, the more their varieties will have changed. With the breakdown of isolation in the modern world, as roads are built and as radio and television enter more and more homes, dialectal variation tends to diminish and languages become more and more homogenized.

Dialectology is the search for spatially and geographically determined differences in various aspects of language. For each village or region that they study, dialectologists want to know the typical local vocabulary or pronunciation. As a result, their subjects of choice are usually older people who have lived all their lives in one location and who have had a minimum of education. Once found, they are quizzed by the fieldworker for names of objects or pronunciations of words or strange expressions.

In the popular wisdom, there is recognition of the 'broad /æ/' of the Yorkshireman, the glottal stop of the Cockney, the Texas drawl, the /r/-less dialect of upper-class Boston. These are **stereotypes**, fixed and prejudicial patterns of thought about people that may be mistaken, but they focus on the most obvious feature of the local accent. There are also obvious differences in lexicon. Peanuts may be called *groundnuts* or *goobers* or *pinders* in different parts of America. There are places in the USA where you buy potatoes in a *bag* and they put your groceries in a *sack*; others where you find potatoes in a *sack* and take your groceries home in a *bag*. Where older dialect terms remain, you might hear *tote* or *poke* or *toot* used instead of *bag* or *sack*.

Careful plotting of these different **variants** permit dialectologists to recognize major regional differences. Thus, the eastern United States has a northern zone where both *grease* and *greasy* are pronounced with an /s/, a transitional zone where *grease* is with an /s/ and *greasy* with a /z/, and a southern where both are /z/. Differences may be quite striking: Texas English, for instance, has one fewer vowel than general American usage, making no difference between the vowel of *pin* and *pen*, so that a Texan is careful to distinguish between a *writing pen* and a *sticking pin*.

In long-settled European countries, dialect atlases show the effects of earlier settlement patterns and of contact. One can trace which areas were originally Celtic, or see evidence of the limits of Roman occupation. In a more recently settled country like the USA, the atlases reveal the differences in original settlement on the Eastern seaboard, showing from what part of England the settlers came and what other linguistic groups they were later mixed with. The US atlases also permit plotting the Western movement of pioneers from the Eastern seaboard along the different pioneering trails.

Geographical differences continue to provide grist for the sociolinguist mill, but the studies have become more complex as the influence of other factors has been accepted. A recent study of the Mexican-American border, for instance, indicates that distance from the border is indeed one of the explanations of Spanish language maintenance among people who have crossed into the United States, but that it needs to be set against other sociological factors such as education and mobility. Geographical space, in other words, is not enough to account for language variation.

This becomes clear if we look at the regular discussion of the difference between a language and a dialect. From a linguistic point of view, regional dialects tend to show minor differences from their immediate neighbours, and greater differences from distant varieties. Thus, one can demonstrate the existence of a chain of dialects from Paris to Rome. At the Franco-Italian border, however, although there is no *linguistic* break in the chain, the *political* distinction is enough to make it clear that one has moved from dialects of French to dialects of Italian.

The decision of what language a dialect belongs to is therefore social and political rather than purely linguistic. As long as Yugoslavia was united, linguists could talk about Serbo-Croatian as a language, with regional variations. With the separation into distinct and warring territories, and with the subsequent transfer of populations and insistence on ethnic difference, Serbian and Croatian have now emerged as distinct languages. In the Netherlands, only Frisian is recognized as a distinct language; all other regional varieties are labelled dialects. A language, it has been remarked, is a dialect with a flag, or even better, with an army. The kinds of differences in patterns of variation that are produced by geographical or spatial isolation are regularly transformed into powerful mechanisms for asserting and recognizing social differences.

4

Styles, gender, and social class

Styles

Geography provides a good beginning when we want to explain language variation. Dialectology is able to account for many of the differences that otherwise play havoc with those who seek a pure, unified language with a single set of correct forms. The differences between *dived* and *dove*, between *footpath* and *pavement,* between /bʌtə/, /bʌʔə/, and /bʌdə/ set difficult quandaries for someone trying to describe *the* English language. Being able to add regional labels to variations helps a great deal. Thus, dictionaries can label forms as *British, American,* or *Australian,* implying the existence of unmarked correct forms.

But even if this is accepted, there remains the issue of variations within individual speakers who come from a single location. Speakers of English sometimes use 'don't' and sometimes use 'do not'. Some Londoners sometimes say /bʌtə/ and at other times say /bʌʔə/. If you carefully record anyone speaking, you will find that there is still patterned variation in the pronunciation of a single phoneme, in the choice of words, and in grammar.

A first useful explanation is provided by the notion of **style** and the related dimension of **formality**. At times, we are more careful, and at times we are more relaxed in our speech or writing, just as at times we are more careful or more relaxed in other kinds of behaviour, like how we dress or eat. This varying level of attention to variety forms a natural continuum, the various levels of which can be divided up in different ways. Each language has its own way of doing this: some, like Javanese or Japanese, have a finely graded set of levels, marked specifically in morphological and lexical choice.

How many distinct points there are on what is really a continuum is not important, but most accounts of language (such as those in good dictionaries and complete grammars) now make some reference to levels of stylistic variation. The cautious writer or speaker is warned in this way how others might react to possible choices, just as etiquette books advise readers how to avoid embarrassment in social settings.

In the sociolinguistic interviews that Labov conducted in the New York City study referred to earlier (see Chapter 1), he found evidence of the informal style (the vernacular he was most interested in) being used when a person he was interviewing interrupted to speak to a child who had entered the room, or offered a cup of coffee to the interviewer, or became excited about the story he or she was telling. In the interview, Labov would elicit more formal use by asking the subject to read a passage or read a list of words. To obtain more casual speech, he asked the subject to tell an emotionally significant story. This gave him three or four levels, and the possibility of comparing changes in certain features at each of them.

In bilingual communities, these stylistic levels may be marked by switching from one variety to another. Officials in Switzerland who use Swiss German in intimate and casual circumstances move to High German for informal and formal speech. Paraguayan city-dwellers switch to Guarani for casual and intimate speech and jokes. Speakers of Arabic who use the vernacular in normal conversation shift to Modern Standard Arabic when they are giving public speeches.

The commonly accepted explanation for this stylistic variation is the care that speakers and writers take with their expression. The more formal the situation, this explanation goes, the more attention we pay to our language and so the more we are likely to conform to the favoured and educated norms of our society. It is in large measure an effect of formal education, especially common where the educational system aims to pass on the prestigious norms associated with literacy.

Attention or care is a good explanation as far as it goes, but it leaves open the question of where the norms come from, and it does not deal with the possibility of conscious choice of a less or more formal style. One explanation for these cases is the idea of

audience design. A speaker who can control more than one variety chooses a level of speech according to the audience he or she is addressing. We might consciously choose an informal style when speaking to strangers in order to seem friendly. Related to this is unconscious **accommodation**; we automatically adjust our speech to be more like that of our interlocutor. Both of these approaches offer some idea of the importance of language in establishing social relations and in representing a speaker's sense of identity, a topic we will explore later in more detail.

It should be noted that this recognition of stylistic levels as being appropriate to specific social situations is in opposition to **normativism**, the approach taken by purists who claim that there is one 'correct' version and that all variation is incorrect and bad. When Webster's Dictionary in its fourth edition introduced stylistic labelling and listed such informal usages as 'ain't', there were many who criticized its admitting the barbarians into the gates of pure English.

Specialized varieties or registers and domains

Dialect concerns variations that are located regionally or socially. Style refers to differences in degree of formality. A third set of variations concerns the special variety (or **register**) especially marked by a special set of vocabulary (technical terminology) associated with a profession or occupation or other defined social group and forming part of its **jargon** or in-group variety. People who work at a particular trade or occupation develop new terms for new concepts. Phrases like *hacking* and *surfing the net* have no obvious meaning to those who are not keeping up with the computer revolution. Terms like a *sticky wicket* and *hit for a six* are understood best by people with some experience of cricket.

A specialized jargon serves not just to label new and needed concepts, but to establish bonds between members of the in-group and enforce boundaries for outsiders. If you cannot understand my jargon, you don't belong to my group. (You might have noticed how in this series of books, the writers are careful to identify new terms by putting them in **bold**, and to explain them in a glossary, all to make it easier for the novice reader to join the group of experts.)

Australian aboriginal secret societies developed their own special forms of language. Thieves and underworld jargons (sometimes called **cant**) are another example. The goal of these was often to make it hard for the outsider to understand conversations. This is not limited to the underworld. In Alsace, where the fact that so many people knew German made Yiddish more widely understandable, Jewish horse traders were reported to have used a great number of Hebrew terms for numbers and parts of a horse so as to keep their language secret. In the course of time, these terms might get known by all professionals in the field, and form part of the register of horse-traders. Gangs and other closed peer groups often develop their own forms of jargon to serve as markers of group membership and also to make their speech less intelligible to outsiders.

Dialects, styles, and registers as we have presented them are ways of labelling varieties of language. The starting point of our classification is the linguistic variation, which we attempt to explain by associating it with a specific set of social features. We might choose to work in the reverse direction, by classifying social situations, and then naming the variety that is suitable for it. A register is a variety of language most likely to be used in a specific situation and with particular roles and statuses involved. Examples might be a toast at a wedding, sports broadcast, or talking to a baby. A register is marked by choices of vocabulary and of other aspects of style.

A useful way of classifying social situations is to analyse them into three defining characteristics: place, role-relationship and topic. Together, these make up a set of typical **domains**. One common domain is *home*. Domains are named usually for a place or an activity in it. Home, then, is the place. The role-relationships associated with home (the people likely to be involved in speech events) include family members (mother, father, son, daughter, grandmother, baby) and visitors. There are a suitable set of topics (depending on the cultural pattern) such as activities of the family, news about family members, the meal, the household. A particular variety of language is appropriate to the domain. In a multilingual community, different languages may well be considered appropriate for different domains. In a multilingual family, different role-relationships might involve different language choice.

For instance, husband and wife might use one language to each other, but father and children might use another.

Another common domain is work. The place might be a factory or an office or a store. The role-relationships include boss, worker, colleague, customer, foreman, client, to mention just a few. The topics are work-related. Now we can understand some of the sociolinguistic complexity that occurs when two people who have one role-relationship at home (such as father and son) have another at work (boss and worker, for instance). When they speak, they can choose a register or language variety to show which relationship is dominant at the time.

Slang and solidarity

The importance of language in establishing social identity is also shown in the case of slang. One way to characterize **slang** is as special kinds of 'intimate' or in-group speech. Slang is a kind of jargon marked by its rejection of formal rules, its comparative freshness and its common ephemerality, and its marked use to claim **solidarity**.

Solidarity, or common group membership, is an important social force that has a major impact on language. The solidarity relations (the claims that we belong to the same group) underlie the notion of accommodation mentioned above. When we are talking to someone, most of us unconsciously move our speech closer to theirs (which explains why our accents change after we have lived in a new place for a long time). Similarly, by choosing the form of language associated with a specific group, we are making a claim to be counted as a member of that group.

This contrasts with the power relation, in which a person's speech carries a claim to be more or less powerful than the other. Slang is primarily speech claiming group membership, and it rejects the power dimensions associated with formal language.

Often, slang is associated with peer group and gang speech, intentionally used to obtain some degree of secrecy. It may be compared to the secret languages found in some tribes. In one Australian aboriginal language, there is a men's society with a secret language in which every word means its opposite. Pig Latin is a children's secret language in which a meaningless vowel is inserted after every syllable. *Canay uyay unayderaystanday thisay?* In southern Arizona, the Spanish-American young people developed a secret variety called *Pachuco* in which they used idioms translated literally from English to Spanish, which couldn't be understood by either their Spanish-speaking elders or their English-speaking fellow students. Cockney rhyming slang (for example, 'titfer' for 'hat,' abbreviated from 'tit for tat') has also been widely publicized.

Slang regularly transgresses other social norms, making free use of taboo expressions. The use of words like 'fuck' and 'shit' in public media has become a mark of liberation or a sign of revolt, depending on one's point of view. But slang also sets up its own norms, the norms of the in-group, so that the gang is easily able to recognize a *lame* or outsider, who does not understand or who misuses slang terms. Slang thus serves social functions, setting and proclaiming social boundaries and permitting speakers to assert or claim membership of identity or solidarity groups. Slang is a feature of the speech of the young and the powerless. Its dynamic nature is partly an effect of the need to develop new in-group terms when slang terms are adopted by other speakers.

Language and gender

All these cases have started to show how language reflects, records, and transmits social differences, so we should not be surprised to find reflexes of gender differences in language, for most societies differentiate between men and women in various marked ways.

Observations of the differences between the way males and females speak were long restricted to grammatical features, such as the differences between masculine and feminine morphology in many languages. In earlier usage, the word **gender** was generally restricted to these grammatical distinctions. They cause problems for speakers of languages like English, where grammatical gender is marked mainly in pronouns, when they learn a language like French, where non-sexed items like table (*la table*) can be grammatically feminine.

It was ethnographers who first drew attention to distinct female and male varieties of language, often with clear differences in vocabulary. The famous anthropologist Levi-Strauss noted how an Amazonian father laughed at his young daughter for using the male word for 'hunting'. Other ethnographers have provided cases of marked differences in the language of men and women. American servicemen in Japan who learned Japanese from the women with whom they associated were thus a source of amusement to people who knew the language.

Historically, these differences sometimes seem to have arisen from customs encouraging marriage outside the community. If there is a regular pattern of men from village A marrying and bringing home to their village women from village B, then it is likely that the speech of women in village A will be marked by many features of the village B dialect. The preservation of these introduced features depends on the maintenance of social differentiation in occupations, status, and activities.

Children soon pick up the social **stereotypes** that underlie this discrimination. They learn that women's talk is associated with the home and domestic activities, while men's is associated with the outside world and economic activities. These prejudices often remain in place in the face of contrary evidence. Thus, while there is a popular prejudice that women talk more than men, empirical studies of a number of social situations (such as committee meetings and Internet discussion groups) have shown the opposite to be true.

There is some intriguingly suggestive evidence of differences in neurophysiological process of aspects of language between males and females. In a recent set of studies using functional magnetic resonance imaging, phonological processing in males was shown to be located in the left half of the brain and in females to involve both left and right parts of the brain. No difference in efficiency was shown, nor is there any evidence so far that any neurophysiological difference accounts for differences between male and female language. The causes are social rather than biological.

Of the social causes of gender differentiation in speech style, one of the most critical appears to be level of education. In all studies, it has been shown that the greater the disparities between educational opportunities for boys and girls, the greater the differences between male and female speech. This can be illustrated with American ultra-orthodox Jewish communities. Males in these communities are expected to spend longer studying traditional

Jewish subjects. Linguistically, this results in their stronger competence in Yiddish and Hebrew, and their weaker control of English. Females on the other hand spend more time on secular studies. While their Hebrew knowledge is much less, their English is much closer to standard. Studies of differences between the speech of Arab men and women also provide evidence that the major cause of difference is educational. In one village, we found greater differences between male and female speech in the half where girls had less education than boys than in the half where both boys and girls had more or less equal opportunity for schooling.

When offered an equal educational opportunity, there seems to be a tendency for women to be more sensitive than men to the status norms of the language. The tendency has been noted in some cities for lower-class males to have much tighter social networks (their neighbours are male relatives, alongside whom they work, and with whom they share leisure hours) and to find their norms within the tight network. The women in these cities have looser multiple networks; they mix more with people outside their community, and so their speech is influenced by the social norms of the wider society.

Studies of gender differences have shown the power of stereotyping. A *poet* is taken more seriously than a *poetess*; women's status is lowered by references to the *girls*. In Hebrew, only the lower ranks in the army (up to the rank of lieutenant) have feminine forms. The use of **generic masculine** ('Everyone should bring *his* lunch, we need to hire the best *man* available'), however well-meaning and neutral the speaker's intention may be, reinforces the secondary status of women in many social groups. With the growth of social awareness in this area over the past decades, there have been many attempts to overcome this prejudicial use of language.

In contrast to the words of the popular saying that 'Sticks and stones may break my bones, but words will never hurt me', it has been shown that **anthropocentric speech** which assumes that men are more important than women is often accompanied by prejudices and actions that do real damage. These usages do not just reflect and record current prejudices, but they are easily transmitted, reinforcing the lower power and prestige ascribed to women in a society. Many publishers and journals now adhere to guidelines to avoid gender stereotyping and gender-prejudiced language use. Everyone should take care with their language.

Exploring the correlations between gender-related linguistic differences and social differences between the genders is another way to see how closely language and social variation are related. But modern societies are divided in other ways too, one of the best studied being social stratification or division into social classes.

Social stratification

While note had been taken earlier of the effect of social class on speech, it was the work of William Labov in New York that established **social stratification**, the study of class distinction in speech, as a major topic in sociolinguistics. Labov himself started out with a purely linguistic question. He wanted to know how, in the terms of the structural linguistics that was in vogue when he was a graduate student, to set up a phonological analysis that included features that were sometimes zero. What were you to do, he asked, in New York City, where speakers sometime pronounced the /r/ after a vowel (post-vocalic /r/) and sometimes didn't? The notion of **free variation**, the notion that the choice of variant was uncontrolled and without significance, was widely used for such cases, but it seemed an unsatisfactory dodging of the question.

He wondered next whether there was any scientifically observable explanation to the variation. In a clever pilot study (see above, page 11), he found that the shop staff (socioeconomically similar in level, but finely varied by the differences in customers and prices) showed regular and predictable variation. The percentage of r-coloration (any tendency to pronounce post-vocalic /r/), he found, correlated closely with the social level of the customers of the store. In fact, in one store, he found a higher percentage of use of the prestige feature among salespeople on the higher, more expensive floors of the store.

In later studies, using extensive interviews with subjects selected on the basis of their socioeconomic classification, the relevance of sociolinguistic evidence to socioeconomic stratification was firmly established. In cities, variations in speech provide clear evidence of social status.

There are historical explanations for social differentiation. The coming of a group of Tewa speakers to the Hopi villages in Arizona explains why the people in the village of Hano were bilingual in Hopi and Tewa, but it was sociocultural and religious differences that accounted for the maintenance of this cleavage for two hundred years. There were similar reasons for the three distinct dialects of Baghdad Arabic, one Christian, one Jewish, and the third Moslem. The different religious groups lived in the same city while maintaining social and cultural isolation.

While historical differences may also be the original cause of social differentiation in large cities (and this is certainly true now as increasingly large groups of immigrants arrive in most cities), there can develop socially marked stratification within a single language. New York is the classic case. Leaving aside the special minority groups (the Blacks and the Hispanics), New Yorkers speak a kind of English that includes the same features, but with certain crucial and socially relevant differences in their distribution. Certain salient phonological variables (such as the *r*-colouring or the pronunciation of [th] or the height of the vowels in *bad* or *off*) vary in all speakers in various situations, with a more standard or prestigious version appearing more often in more formal speech. Thus, the pattern for lower middle-class speakers in New York was to use the stigmatized /t/ or /tθ/ pronunciations only occasionally in very careful speech reading word lists, to use it about 20% of the time in careful speech, and to use it 30% of the time in casual speech.

Each social level (as determined on the basis of income, occupation, and education) had a similar gradation according to style or degree of formality. But there were also marked differences between the social levels. In casual speech, for instance, the upper-middle class would use a stigmatized form about 10% of the time, the lower-middle class about 20%, the working class about 80%, and the lower class about 90%. Thus, the same feature differentiated the stylistic level and the social level.

In practice, these fairly fine differences, which affect only a small part of speech and do not interfere with intelligibility, help New Yorkers to identify themselves and each other socially. Sometimes they do this even more subtly and sensitively than do more obvious socioeconomic markers like income and education.

There are social forces leading to or delaying the diffusion. One striking observation was a tendency in the upwardly mobile and socially insecure lower-middle class to over-use (relative to the normal slope) socially desirable features in very careful speech and reading. This **hypercorrection** suggests that the feature is recognized as a stereotype rather than still serving as an unconscious social marker.

The analyses we have discussed to date of these variations have depended on associating linguistic features (for example, the percentage of r-coloration) with social or demographic factors (gender, educational level, socioeconomic status). As far as it goes, the explanatory power of these correlations appears good, but correlation and causation are not the same thing. We obtain a more powerful account of what is involved if we add social psychological factors like attitude and accommodation, and consider them as causes.

Accommodation and audience design

How is it that dialect differences and stylistic differences emerge? The simplest solution is that people tend to talk like the people they talk to most of the time. The physical isolation of villages explains why their dialects are different from the dialects of neighbouring villages, and even more different from those of more distant villages and towns. Similarly, the social isolation of specific groups explains why their languages or dialects remain relatively unaffected by that of other groups. It was because the religious groups in Baghdad had limited contact with each other that the Christians, Moslems, and Jews there maintained distinctive dialects. It was the social distance between the castes in an Indian village that led to differences in their speech.

An alternative suggestion is to consider the driving force as **audience design**, a concept mentioned earlier on page 33. In this view, the speaker, consciously or not, chooses a stylistic level appropriate for the audience he or she wishes to address. The notion comes from radio announcers, who suit their style to their audience. The same announcer will be found to have distinct styles when reading a news item on a national station and when introducing a song on a popular music station. By selecting a style appropriate to a particular audience, the announcer is identifying himself or herself with the audience or claiming membership of the group that it constitutes.

Adding this social dimension increases the explanatory power. One speaks most like the people with whom one regularly associates, but one may also choose, in appropriate circumstances, to allow one's speech to move in the direction of another group. As we noted earlier, many speech sounds are not always pronounced in the same way by the same speaker, but their realizations form rather a pattern not unlike the patterns of bullet or arrow hits on a target. While there may be a rare bull's-eye, the shots as a whole form a more or less consistent group. If one moves one's aim, the whole group moves, with the centre changing.

In conversations between people with differing pronunciation, it has been noticed that there is a common tendency for the pronunciation of the two to move slightly closer together. This process, called **accommodation**, explains the way that a person who moves to a new part of the country gradually modifies his or her speech in the direction of the new norm. Because we are talking about changes in probabilities and percentages, the change need not be immediately obvious to the speaker or the listener. But if we record a conversation between two speakers of differing varieties, we find that their percentage of use of some features often converge. It is common to find that your speech—choice of vocabulary, grammatical forms, and even pronunciation—moves towards that of your interlocutor.

The opposite effect also occurs, when a speaker chooses not to converge but to diverge, by moving his or her speech away from the other party. Rather than converging, one may choose to stress features that connect one not to the other person present, but to an absent but valued hypothetical audience, such as a peer group or an admired outsider. We have already mentioned the same phenomenon in the use of non-standard slang for showing in-group membership.

This powerful sociolinguistic phenomenon would seem related to the most fundamental linguistic features involved in social bonding. Just as two speakers talking together tend to be moving in the same rhythm, so they unconsciously adapt their speech to accommodate to each other. It is this sympathetic movement and its absence that enable a speaker easily to pick out which members of his or her audience are not listening.

The same factor also accounts for the tendency to speak like one's friends and peers, and to modify one's speech either in their direction, or to some other socially desirable prestige group. Consciously and unconsciously, one uses one's speech, through selection among socially labelled variants which need not change meaning or interfere with intelligibility, to express a claim of solidarity and social group membership. In an early study of the speech of high-school students on Martha's Vineyard, an island off the New England coast, it was shown that the height of their /æ/ (as pronounced in words like *cat* and *mat*) signalled either their intention to live the rest of their life on the island, or their desire to move to the mainland.

The existence of variation in language, therefore, is not accidental or meaningless. It adds a vital set of social dimensions, making it possible for language to reflect and record an individual's demographic, geographic, sociological, educational, and religious background. It helps constitute identity; it claims solidarity; it expresses attitudes towards power and prestige. This rich complexity helps us understand both how and why language changes, for the social forces injected into variation provide the dynamism of change.

The possibility of using variation in language to identify group membership can have harmful effects, when it is associated with prejudice. Telephone operators at car factories in Detroit were reported to be trained to recognize Afro-Americans by their speech and to say there were no jobs available. Where there is prejudice against foreigners or members of a social class, speaking a stigmatized variety can do serious harm. In a study in New York, adding non-standard features to a taped sample of a voice led listeners to lower their judgement of the employability of a speaker. The more stratified a society, the more likely it is that speaking a prestige variety will be rewarded, and that speaking a non-standard variety will lead to prejudicial treatment.

While it is possible, as we have seen, to recognize factors like these through the study of variation with a single language variety, they are even more salient when two or more languages are involved. In the next chapter we will look at bilinguals and bilingualism.

5
Bilinguals and bilingualism

Language socialization

Children acquire language and social skills together. Their sensitivity to the social uses of languages is already apparent in their early learning of different varieties. Even while they are still in the babbling stage, many children have a different way of addressing small objects (animals, toys, other babies) from the way they address adults. If they do this, they are showing that they have learned that babies are talked to using a different variety. This register that is used to speak to babies is called **baby talk**, and has been shown to occur in many languages. From an early age, children learn that there is more than one variety of language.

There are in fact a vast set of social rules about language that a child must acquire to be successfully socialized. One is the rule for conversational organization. Knowing when to speak and when to be silent, how to enter a conversation, when to speak quietly, and when clearly, are all part of the conversational rules that children have to learn. Equally confusing at first are the pragmatic rules, such as comprehending that a question may be a request. We may be frustrated when speaking to child on the phone. 'Yes!' he answers when we ask 'Is your mother there?', making no effort to fetch her. Children have to learn the social conventions for language use. Learning these social conventions is a key component of socialization.

One of the most revealing opportunities for studying language socialization is in the case of children growing up bilingually, for they manage not just to keep the two languages separate, but to learn quickly which language to use to which person. They also realize which people can be addressed in a mixture of the two languages. In this way, bilingual children can be said to develop control over three distinct varieties of language. The study of bilingualism provides an excellent laboratory for learning how a child can learn to be a member of two (or more) distinct societies.

The description of bilingualism

While it is the case that even speakers of a single language (putative monolinguals) control various styles and levels of that language, it is very common that people develop some knowledge and ability in a second language and so become **bilingual**. The simplest definition of a bilingual is a person who has some functional ability in a second language. This may vary from a limited ability in one or more domains, to very strong command of both languages (which is sometimes called **balanced bilingualism**). The assumption that there must be a single definition leads to confusion, such as when one person is talking about the highly skilled multiple-domained balanced bilingualism of an expert translator and interpreter, and the other the uneven skills of a recent immigrant. Additional confusion is caused by the common use of the term bilingual to refer to a socially disfavoured minority group: in Texas, for instance, it is restricted to Mexican-Americans.

Rather than worrying about definition, it is more useful to consider what is needed to describe the nature of an individual's bilingualism. Clearly, the first (and not necessarily easy) element is to identify each of the languages. We will often need to clarify which variety is involved: to distinguish between Cantonese and *Putonghoa,* or between Egyptian and Moroccan Arabic, or between High German and Swiss German.

A second important feature is the way each language was acquired. It is useful to distinguish between mother (or native) tongue learning, second (or informal) language learning, and foreign (or additional) language learning. Each of these suggest different possible kinds of proficiency. It is useful also to note the age of learning and the time spent using the language. We describe two bilinguals in this way: 'X is a native speaker of Cantonese and learned English in school.' 'Y grew up speaking Moroccan Arabic, but was educated in French and has lived in Paris since the age of 15.'

Another set of distinctions is that of skill—reading, writing, speaking, understanding speech. It is not uncommon for people to speak one language and read and write another. Many Navajos use their own language in conversation, but read in English. Until the literacy campaigns of recent times, Ethiopians who spoke Amharic were more likely to read Gi'iz than Amharic. The receptive skills of reading and understanding speech are often stronger in a learned language than are the productive skills of speaking and writing. Many people obtain reading knowledge of a language at school, but cannot speak it.

In describing the bilingualism of an individual, another set of differences is often evident in the performance of certain internal functions. Bilinguals usually prefer one language for functions such as counting, doing arithmetic, dreaming (some people dream in language, others don't), cursing, or praying silently.

Another useful way to describe bilinguals is by describing the external functions they can perform in each language. These might be expressed as 'can-do' statements: X can read a daily newspaper, can carry on an informal conversation, can give a lecture. One special ability (not true in the case of all bilinguals) is the skill of translation from one language to the other. Another useful approach to describe a bilingual's language use is by domains rather than by functions.

A domain, as we have discussed above on page 34, is an empirically determined cluster consisting of a location, a set of role-relationships, and a set of topics. Just as this notion was useful for identifying the use of registers, so it is useful for considering bilingualism. For each of the domains, a bilingual is likely to have a preferred language. Some examples of domains are shown in Table 5.1.

Bilinguals have a repertoire of domain-related rules of language choice. The home–school or the home–work switch is probably the most common, with one language learned at home from parents and the second learned at school and used at work. When there is a language shift in progress, certain traditional domains may remain favoured for the use of one language. For the Maori people, before the recent language revival activities began, the *marae* where traditional ceremonies and meetings took place remained the strongest bastion of Maori language use. The bilingualism we mentioned earlier in Swiss adults is domain-related, with High German used in the work domain and Swiss German in the home and neighbourhood. In his study of Puerto Ricans in New Jersey, Fishman noted strong Spanish maintenance in home, neighbourhood, and church, and strong English usage at school and at work. It is normal for immigrants to continue to use their original language in the home and in religious domains, while using the new language in work, education, and public domains.

Location	Role-relationships	Topics
Home	Mother, father, son, daughter, etc.	Domestic, personal, etc.
Neighbourhood	Neighbour, shop-keeper, street-cleaner	Weather, shopping, social greetings
School	Teacher, student, principal	Social greetings, educational
Church	Priest, parishioner, etc.	Sermons, prayers, confession, social

TABLE 5.1

Because domains are composite concepts, there is the possibility of conflict and therefore marked choice between languages. Thus, two people who normally speak the standard language at work might use their home language there to signal either a change of role-relation (family member or friend rather than co-worker) or topic (a home or neighbourhood topic) while still being in the some location. We shall take this up again later when we talk about switching. At this point, the important notion is that a bilingual's use of his or her two languages is likely to vary considerably according to domain.

Bilingual competence

We have been describing so far the language use or **performance** of a bilingual. The description makes clear why it is that it is rare to find equal ability in both languages. Assume a bilingual immigrant who grew up speaking Language A, but was educated formally in Language B. Such a person might well have all the conversational skills in Language A, but be quite weak at dealing with academic matters in it. Misunderstanding of this possible difference in **competence** often leads to educational problems: teachers might assume, for instance, that a child who has reasonable conversational ability also has the full basis for academic work in the language.

The nature of bilingual competence is a topic of considerable interest and importance for the psycholinguist as well as the sociolinguist. How are the two languages organized in the bilingual brain? For a number of years, there was an attempt to distinguish between **compound bilinguals** whose two languages were assumed to be closely connected, because one language had been learned after (and so through) the other, and **co-ordinate bilinguals** who had learned each language in separate contexts, and so kept them distinct. Over-simplifying, co-ordinate bilinguals were assumed to have two meaning systems each with its own set of words, while compounds had a single system with two sets of words.

Co-ordinate

English concept 'table'	Navajo concept 'table'
English word 'table'	Navajo word *bikáá adaáni*

Compound

Mixed concept 'table'	
English word 'table'	Navajo word *bikáá adaáni*

The problem that a compound bilingual would face is that the two words in fact refer to a different set of concepts. Underlying this is the question of whether for the bilingual the knowledge of the two languages develops independently or together. The notion of domain difference suggests the different kinds of experiences most bilinguals have in each of their languages, implying a common core of knowledge with subsequent differentiation. Recent neurolinguistic research suggests that paired words are stored in the same place in the brains of those who are bilingual from infancy, but in non-overlapping places in those who develop bilingualism later.

However explained neurophysiologically, the phenomenon of bilingualism is the prime example of **language contact,** for the two languages are in contact in the bilingual. This contact can lead to **interference**. A compound bilingual who has learned the meaning of words in another language by attaching them to the words of his or her first language demonstrates semantic interference. There can be interference in all aspects of a language, from the sound system (having an 'accent') to conversational rules (interrupting or saying 'please' in the wrong way).

The phenomenon of interference, especially when it involves using the two languages together, has led to the study of code switching.

Code switching and code mixing

Bilinguals often switch between their two languages in the middle of a conversation. These code-switches can take place between or even within sentences, involving phrases or words or even parts of words. The switching of words is the beginning of **borrowing,** which occurs when the new word becomes more or less integrated into the second language. One bilingual individual using a word from language A in language B is a case of switching, but when many people do, even speakers of B who don't know A are likely to pick it up. At this stage, especially if the pronunciation and morphology have been adapted, we can say the word has been borrowed.

There are various kinds of **code switching**. Immigrants often use many words from their new language in their old language, because many of the people they speak to know both languages. In situations like this, bilinguals often develop a **mixed code**. In such a case, we might want to distinguish between code switching of the two languages and the mixed variety. The history of English shows many such mixed codes, as first Danish and later Norman words were added by bilinguals. The various contemporary Englishes, such as Jamaican English or New Zealand English, can be seen as mixed codes, with the addition of local lexicon as their most obvious feature.

For a bilingual, shifting for convenience (choosing the available word or phrase on the basis of easy availability) is commonly related to topic. Showing the effect of domain differences, a speaker's vocabulary will develop differentially for different topics in the two languages. Thus, speakers of a language who have received advanced education in a professional field in a second language will usually not have the terms in their native language. Scientists trained in an English-speaking country giving university lectures in their own language often mix in English words or even switch to English phrases and sentences.

More interesting effects are achievable by shifts concerned with role-relationships. It is important to note that each of a bilingual's languages is likely to be associated not just with topics and places, but also with identities and roles associated with them. In the midst of speaking about work matters in Language A, a sentence or two in Language B will be able to show that the two speakers are not just fellow-employees but also fellow members of an ethnic group. The use of tags and expressions from Language B while speaking Language A enables a speaker to make this kind of identity claim easily. This kind of shift, called **metaphorical switching**, is a powerful mechanism for signalling social attitudes or claiming group membership or solidarity.

The selection of a language by a bilingual, especially when speaking to another bilingual, carries a wealth of social meaning. Each language becomes a virtual guise for the bilingual speaker, who can change identity as easily as changing a hat, and can use language choice as a way of negotiating social relations with an interlocutor.

The bilingual individual thus provides a rich field for sociolinguistic study. A full understanding of bilingualism, however, depends on a deeper understanding of the nature of the speech communities in which they operate. In the next chapter we will look at societal multilingualism.

6

Societal multilingualism

Multilingualism

The discussion of speech communities and repertoires in Chapter 2 foreshadowed our detailed consideration of the interest that sociolinguists take in bilingual and multilingual societies. Bilingualism and multilingualism, whether in an individual speaker or in a social group, are the most obvious and salient cases of variation to observe. With stylistic or dialectal variation, identifying each variety is harder and open to dispute, but with distinctly recognized languages, there is generally agreement on the varieties and their names. We can study how two or more languages intertwine and separate without first being forced, as we are when we talk about stylistic variations within a single language, to establish the criteria for difference. It is both the salience and the commonness of multilingualism that has led to its being so well studied.

Monolingual speech communities are rare; monolingual countries are even rarer. Even a country as linguistically homogeneous as Japan has its linguistic minorities like the Ainu and the Koreans, marginalized as they might be. True, many countries have developed an explicit or implicit language policy as though they were monolingual, but it is rare (and becoming rarer) for linguistic and national borders not to overlap in various complex ways. Most countries have more than one language that is spoken by a significant portion of the population, and most languages have significant numbers of speakers in more than one country.

Historically, multilingual communities evolve in a number of ways. One is as a result of migration, the voluntary or involuntary movements of people speaking one language into the territory of people speaking another. When the Hopi Indians permitted or encouraged a group of Tewa Indians to move from the Rio Grande area to the Arizonan mesas (each group has a different version of the story), they produced a bilingual village, Hano, among nine that were Hopi-speaking. Mutual distrust and a ban on intermarriage that lasted into the beginning of the twentieth century kept the villages socially distinct. Later, the bilingual villagers of Hano added Spanish and Navajo to their language repertoires, and after the introduction of Bureau of Indian Affairs schools, joined the rest of the Hopi in shifting towards English use.

Involuntary migration or forced movement of population was common in the ancient Middle East, as is recorded in the Biblical account of the Babylonian exile, and has continued to be a significant force accounting for multilingual communities. In the nineteenth century, the British policy of bringing indentured Indian workers to the Fijian sugar plantations led to Fiji's current division between speakers of the indigenous Fijian dialects and Hindi-speaking descendants of the original plantation workers. The African slave trade moved large numbers of native speakers of different languages into the East and West Indies, and led to the formation of the pidgins and creoles (to be discussed in a later section). In the twentieth century, the Soviet policy of forced movement of populations assured that many of the newly independent post-Soviet countries are saddled with a challenging multilingual problem. In the Baltic states, it is the Russian immigrants, once the rulers, who are faced with the challenge to learn the now dominant Estonian, Latvian, and Lithuanian.

In the years after the Second World War, Northern European countries, too, enhanced their multilingualism by encouraging guest workers from the Mediterranean areas. There are significant Turkish minorities in many parts of Europe, and Greek, Spanish, Algerian, and Italian immigrants moved north in the same way. In a response to the social and linguistic problems produced, a new Norwegian multilingual policy is intended to cope with (and encourage the maintenance of) nearly a hundred languages.

Voluntary migration has produced major changes in the

linguistic make-up of many countries in the world. While some of its multilingualism was produced in other ways, the United States, as the world's foremost receiver of voluntary immigration, grew quickly into a multilingual society, constantly assimilating large numbers of the immigrants through a melting-pot policy. In the nineteenth and early twentieth century, the United States absorbed large communities of speakers of German, Norwegian, Greek, Italian, Yiddish, Polish, Ukrainian, Japanese, various Chinese languages, and Spanish. The rate of absorption was slowed down after 1923, when strict immigration laws were passed. There was some relaxation of this policy in the post-war period, including an influx of South East Asian speakers of Vietnamese, Cambodian, Laotian, and other languages, and a recent wave of immigrants from the former Soviet Union. Most of these groups have acquired English, and many have given up on their traditional languages. Throughout this period, continued immigration, legal and illegal, especially of Spanish speakers, and the rise of ethnic awareness have been threatening to upset this comfortable monolingual trend.

Migration from the countryside or from small towns to the large metropolitan cities that have grown everywhere in the twentieth century is another major cause of multilingual communities. In the Third World as much as in the developed countries, this movement to the cities is creating huge megalopolises, conurbations with populations in the millions, attracting complex patterns of multilingualism, and producing major problems for social, economic, and political development. As African cities expand at an ever-increasing rate, they too become highly multilingual.

Multilingualism has also historically been created by conquest and the subsequent incorporation of speakers of different languages into a single political unit. The incorporation of Brittany, Alsace, and Provence into France submerged the languages of these regions. The spread of English power over the British Isles produced multilingualism and lead to the loss of some Celtic languages. The growth of the Russian empire under the Czars, continued under Soviet rule, made the Soviet Union a multilingual country. The conquest of Central and South America by the Spaniards and Portuguese eventually produced countries with large indigenous minorities, some still speaking many Indian languages. The occupation of New Mexico and Texas and the incorporation of Puerto Rico by the growing United States included new Spanish-speaking populations within territorial limits.

Colonial policies also led to multilingual states. While the Moslem Empire largely replaced the indigenous languages with Arabic, pockets of multilingualism remained—the Kurds in Turkey, Iraq, and Syria, the Aramaic speakers in Syria, the Copts in Egypt, the Berbers in Algeria and Morocco, to mention a few—and the language mixes led to the great variations in the spoken Arabic dialects held together by the general acceptance of an overarching Classical Arabic. When Spain conquered Latin America, it created countries where Spanish dominated a mixture of marginalized indigenous varieties, including some, like Mayan, that had previously had their turn as the dominant language in a multilingual empire.

When the major European powers divided up Africa in the nineteenth century, they drew boundaries that left most post-independence states without a single majority language, and usually with languages that had many speakers outside as well as inside the new state borders. They thus opened the way, wittingly or not, for a tendency to adopt the colonial government's metropolitan language as a needed *lingua franca*. Newly independent states like India, Pakistan, Indonesia, and Singapore also faced complex language policy decisions that were heavily weighted with effects of colonial policies.

Many of these former colonies might be considered cases of forced federation. More rarely, there has been voluntary federation. One classic case is Switzerland where speakers of French, German, Italian, and Romansch formed a multilingual state. Another is Belgium, where Walloon speakers of various French dialects, Flemish speakers of various Dutch dialects, and some speakers of German dialects added to the package, now form an uncomfortable but working French-Dutch bilingual state. Other federations, like the Serbo-Croatian union in Yugoslavia, or the Czech-Slovak union, brought into existence in the halcyon days of the post-First World War spirit of tolerant democracy and held in place in the post-Second World War period by Soviet power, have proved to be unstable after the collapse of the Soviet empire.

These diverse historical circumstances have produced many different kinds of multilingual mixes, sometimes stable and sometimes volatile and short-lived. The most common result of this **language contact** has been **language conflict**, producing pressure from one language on speakers of other languages to adopt it. This pressure, whether the conscious result of a planned policy or the effect of a multitude of unplanned factors, has produced challenges to social structure that many people have begun to worry about. The study of **language maintenance** and of **language shift** has thus become a central concern of sociolinguists interested in multilingual societies.

Language loyalty and reversing language shift

Many people nowadays have become troubled by the extinction of various species of animals and birds, and lists of endangered species are regularly publicized. Linguists have noticed that languages too are in danger of dying, and for some time have been studying **language loyalty**, the ability (or lack of it) of speakers of a language to stand up to the pressure of more powerful languages. They have expressed distress at the threatened fate of **endangered languages**, languages that are no longer being passed on to children as native languages, but are spoken by a contracting and aging group of adults.

One early major study looked at what happened to the immigrant and indigenous languages of the United States when faced by the inexorable power of English. Most American immigrant languages were slowly sapped of their strength as younger speakers shifted to English not just in the public domains, but also in their own community and homes. Some factors appeared to speed up the process or slow it down. The greatest resistance to language shift was found in groups that chose to isolate themselves both linguistically and culturally from the mainstream. Two clear cases were isolationist Mennonite Christian groups (especially Hutterian and Old Order Amish) and the ultra-orthodox Hassidic Jews, both of whom rejected not just the language but also the dress and social conduct of their new country. In these cases, the isolation was self-imposed.

A second group that maintained their languages were those

who were segregated and isolated by the outside society and whose access to the easy social mobility that other immigrants enjoyed was obstructed by social discrimination. The clearest cases here were the indigenous Native Americans and the various Spanish-speaking indigenous and immigrant groups. When they were denied access to jobs, housing, and education, they were at the same time cut off from easy access to the English that was assumed to be the way to assimilation.

Language shift has been studied in many parts of the world. There are groups that have worked actively to reverse the seemingly inevitable language shift that occurs when small weak languages, or the languages of marginalized groups, come into contact with large powerful languages used and favoured by the majority or dominant group. There have been many attempts to correct this loss of linguistic diversity. A commonly cited case is the national effort to revive the use of Irish in Ireland, a nationalistically inspired and state-supported initiative to preserve Irish in the western areas (the *Gaeltacht*) where it was still spoken, and to teach it through the schools in the other areas where there were few speakers left. In the English-speaking areas, students continue to learn Irish at school, but to use it very little outside school or afterwards. Even in the *Gaeltacht* there has been a continued loss, largely because of the failure to combine social and economic planning with linguistic. At first, the continuing poverty of the area led Irish speakers to move away to the cities or emigrate, in both cases switching to English; later, economic development plans brought in English speakers looking for jobs.

More successful was the **revitalization** of Hebrew, a strong ideologically based process realized between 1890 and 1914, mainly in Ottoman Palestine, by returning Zionists who were looking to build a new nation using an old language. In agricultural settlements, in new towns like Tel Aviv, and in communal settlements, Hebrew was revitalized. It had the component of **vitality** or natural intergenerational transmission restored after some 1700 years during which it had only been learned as an additional language. Building on the widespread knowledge of the continually enriched written language, and driven by the force of their ideological commitments, the revivers were successful in establishing modern Hebrew as the language used for all purposes in Israel today.

Activities aimed at **reversing language shift** are sometimes private and small (as with the few hundred enthusiasts working to revive the Cornish language) but often public and political. The efforts to save French language, culture, and identity in Quebec threaten to divide the province from the rest of Canada. In Spain, the post-Franco policy of granting semi-autonomy to the regions has led to strong government-supported campaigns for Basque and Catalan. In the Baltic States, the collapse of the Soviet Union has permitted the restoration of the power of Estonian, Latvian, and Lithuanian. We shall return to discuss this issue later when we talk of language planning and policy.

Language and ethnic identity

Why does multilingualism and language contact entail so much emotional reaction? The answer lies not in the practical communicative realm, but in the symbolic function of languages and varieties. One of the most common ways of identifying a person is by his or her language. Because language is inherently involved in socialization, the social group whose language you speak is an important identity group for you. There are other markers of ethnic identity, such as food or clothing or religion. But language has a special role, in part because it organizes thought and in part because it establishes social relations.

Multilingual societies inevitably face conflict over language choice. Some aspects of concern for language choice can be explained practically, politically, or economically. The speakers of a language are in a stronger position when their language is used for national or international communication, or for government, or for trade and commerce, or for education. But the role of language in establishing social identity adds an additional, non-material dimension to the conflict.

Ethnic groups regularly use language as one of their most significant identifying features. There are some groups, like the Frisians in the north of the Netherlands, who are hard put to find other features that distinguish them from their neighbours. Commonly, the name of an ethnic group and its language are the same. Most ethnic groups believe that their language is the best medium for preserving and expressing their traditions.

One of the paradoxical effects of this connection of language and ethnicity may be understood by looking at the case of post-Franco Spain. With the granting of some degree of autonomy to the provinces, Catalan and Basque have once again been recognized as official languages in their own autonomous regions. The result of this new territorial policy has been to create problems for people who are ethnically Basque or Catalan but live outside the regions, and for people who are Castilian speakers but live within them.

As we will note in the next section, conflict over choice of language often accompanies the development of a new nation.

Language and politics

Language is regularly used in the exercise of political power. A government can attempt to control its minority groups by banning their language, as Turkey bans the use of Kurdish by one its larger minorities. By requiring that voting material be made available in Spanish and other minority languages, the US Federal Voting Act tried to increase minority participation in government. By offering extra pay to federal Civil Servants who knew both English and French, the Canadian government attempted to weaken the demand for Quebec separatism. By requiring all its citizens to pass examinations in Estonian, Latvian, or Lithuanian, the newly independent Baltic states attempted to redress the balance of power for indigenous citizens over the large Russian minority populations that were dominant during the period of Soviet rule. The issue of language choice is most critical in the case of a newly independent state, as will be discussed in the next chapter.

There are more subtle uses of language in politics. The use of a regional or a social dialect by a political leader is often a claim to a specialized ethnic identity. South American politicians sometimes claim greater regional identity by using more Indian features in their Spanish. Labour Party politicians in England have sometimes used regional accents to mark a dissociation from middle-class speech and values. Anwar Sadat backed away from Pan-Arabism by using more Egyptian vernacular in his speech when the norm for Arab public speech is the Classical language.

Language rights

The issue of language or linguistic rights provides an opportunity to attempt to take an ethical rather than a scientific view of language contact and conflict. There are a number of possible approaches. One, favoured by some linguists, puts emphasis on the right of a language, like any other endangered species, to survive. Because every language incorporates some unique features derived from the rich and varied experience of human beings, **language loss** (i.e. the loss of all its speakers) is held to be as serious as the loss of an animal or bird species. There are two possible ways of dealing with this. Most commonly, anthropological linguists have worked to preserve, in a grammar, dictionary, and collections of texts, as much of the language as possible while there is still one speaker alive. More recently, linguists have provided support to the speakers of the language in their efforts at reversing language shift.

The second approach is to focus not on the rights of the language as an abstraction but on the rights of the speakers of the language. Here, we may distinguish between the rights of the speakers of a language to use it, and their rights to maintain it by teaching it to their children.

The first of these issues concerns the rights of linguistic minorities or of individuals who do not speak the national or official languages of a political unit. To the extent that a state recognizes the right of its citizens and other inhabitants to access to work, health care, housing, education, justice, and democracy, so it must take care to deal with the potential lessening or blocking of these rights for those who do not speak, read, or write the official or national language or languages. There are several ways this right may be recognized. One is the provision of adequate instruction in the official or national language or languages to all who do not control it—not just children, but new immigrants and temporary foreign workers. A second is the provision of interpreting and translating services to those who have not yet had the opportunity to learn the national language. This first language right, therefore, is the right to learn the national language, and in the meantime, to be assisted in dealing with those situations where lack of control of it leads to serious handicaps.

A second right is not to be discriminated against, in access to work, education, justice, or health service, on the basis of being identified as a member of a group speaking another language or variety. This refers to the way in which linguistic minority members, however competent they may be in the standard language, are often classified as 'bilinguals' and afforded lower status. It also refers to the way in which speakers of an unfavoured dialect or accent or other variety of a language are automatically recognized as 'different' on linguistic grounds, and discriminated against. It should be noted that this right is part of the larger right not to be discriminated against on the basis of group membership, religion, gender, ethnic group, or other factors irrelevant to the matter being decided.

A third right concerns the right of a group of speakers of a language to preserve and maintain their own favoured language or variety, and to work to reverse any language shift to the status or prestige variety. Here, there are some more complex issues. One is the potential conflict between the rights of individuals and groups. A group may wish to preserve its language, but individual members may prefer to shift to the dominant language, which is generally a language more able to deal with modern life and economic success. Another is the issue of who should pay for the reverse shift efforts. Should it be the language community, and should it be provided outside the regular school system? Examples of this are the Greek and Chinese afternoon schools in the USA and some other countries, the Jewish Day School movement that has grown up in the USA, Canada, Australia, Latin America, and elsewhere, and the international schools that operate in many countries. Or should it be the state, in programmes to provide bilingual education to as many minority groups as possible? In this issue of linguistic minorities, it is generally accepted that indigenous minorities, like the Native Americans in the United States, have a higher claim to maintaining language, religion, and culture, than do immigrant groups who came by choice.

Considering language rights takes us into major issues of language policy, which will be dealt with in Chapter 7.

Pidgins and creoles

A second aspect of language contact is the development of distinct varieties of language. A **pidgin** language is one that evolves in circumstances where there are limited relations between the speakers of different languages, such as a market, or where there is a special situation of power relations, being typical of the kind of master–slave relation on a plantation. It is a variety of language that is marked by the fact that it is not a native language of anyone, but is learned only in contact by people who normally continue to speak their own language inside their own community. The complexity of a pidgin varies according to the communicative demands placed on it; as there are increasing functional demands, there is a growth in the power and complexity of the pidgin to meet them.

A pidgin is a social rather than an individual solution. There are cases where individual speakers acquire only a limited control of a language in which they need to do business. Such, for instance, was the limited knowledge of Navajo developed by white traders. Each speaker made his own mistakes and compromises. The term 'pidgin' is better kept for social varieties with established norms.

A pidgin involves the mixture of two or more languages. Sometimes, the grammatical system is based more or less on one language and the vocabulary is largely taken from another. In all cases, the grammar is simplified, that is to say certain features of the base language are dropped. Many different pidgins have been identified and described, including, to name a few, Nigerian Pidgin English, Papuan Pidgin English, Vietnamese Pidgin French, New Guinea Pidgin German, Kenya Pidgin Swahili, Fanalago (a pidgin based on Zulu), and Chinook Jargon.

In many social circumstances, pidgins have become quite stable over time. Spoken only as second languages, and functioning in limited domains as **languages of wider communication**, they are learned informally in contact and used especially as trade languages. In multilingual areas where each of the existing language groups maintain their distinctiveness and do not intermarry, the pidgin continues.

In many cases, there is a further development. This occurs when, as a result of intermarriage of a couple whose native languages are different but who both speak pidgin, the pidgin is spoken at home and learned by children as a first or mother tongue. In the terms of contemporary linguistic theory, this leads to some fundamental changes. Children acquiring the language do so in the same way that children acquire any other language, and it is believed that this involves the same appeal to innate linguistic capacity and universals that accounts for first language acquisition. New features emerge as a result both of this and of the growing complexity of the social circumstances in which the language is used. It is no longer just a contact language, with limited social functions, but is called on to deal with an increasingly wide range of social needs. The process is called **creolization**, as the language expands and develops, displaying greater phonological and grammatical complexity.

Some of the better-described creoles are Haitian Creole, Tok Pisin (a creolized version of a New Guinea Pidgin English), and Hawaiian Creole English; some of the most recently recognized include Berbice Creole Dutch and Palanquero (Colombian Creole Spanish). These creoles appear to have much the same grammatical complexity as other natural languages, although they of course show many of the characteristics of their original pidgin status, such as the blended phonology, and the existence of two or more grammatical and lexical bases.

A third stage of development can occur when speakers of a creole or pidgin are introduced, usually by education, to the standard language on which the creole or pidgin was originally based. There can ensue what has been labelled a **post-creole continuum**, in which the various levels of social and stylistic variation may be filled by a version of the standard language at the upper end and of the creole or pidgin at the lower end. A Jamaican may, in various social situations, choose the creole called Jamaica Talk or one of the various intermediate levels, or a standard Jamaican version of English, or may switch from one to the other as in other kinds of code switching.

One controversy in sociolinguistics has been over the origin of the variety of English associated with the speech of Afro-Americans. For many years, it was assumed to be a non-Standard social dialect, similar to and based on the Southern regional dialects of American English, and reflecting the social isolation and inadequate education of the former slaves. Some psychologists pointed to certain features, such as the absence of the copula (the verb 'to be') in the present tense, or different rules of verb agreement, or the use of the double negative, as evidence of linguistic inferiority and therefore justification for discrimination against speakers of the variety. Linguists pointed out that these features are common in standard languages (Russian and Hebrew do not use a copula in the present tense, French negatives are usually double), and show that these and other features support a theory that **Black English**, as they labelled it, derives from an original creole like the Gullah still spoken in some communities. From this, others argued for its status as a separate language, and called for its recognition and maintenance. The controversy over what is variously called Black English, Afro-American Vernacular English, or Ebonics has raged in American educational situations for at least thirty years.

Because of their lack of formal recognition, pidgins and creoles are often treated just as a local jargon and linguistic aberration. It is only recently that they have become an area of great interest to linguists interested to learn about universal tendencies in languages and to study language status, attitudes to language, and the importance of language to group identity. There are still many controversies about how to describe them and how to explain their creation and development. But it is their very marginality that makes them interesting to sociolinguistics, for they are most open to social influences and, lacking academies and educational establishments, the least likely to be formalized and restricted by normativistic rule-making.

Diglossia

A third aspect of language contact relates to the issue of functional allocation. With a handful of languages, two distinct varieties of the same language are used, side by side, for two different sets of functions. The term **diglossia** (modelled on the word *bilingual*, and using Greek rather than Latin forms) was coined originally to label this phenomenon. In the Arabic-speaking world, there is the contrast between the Classical language and regional dialect. The same pattern, more or less, occurs in the German-speaking cantons of Switzerland with High German as the standard language and Swiss German as the vernacular, in Haiti with French and Haitian Creole, and in Greece with the literary variety, *katharévusa,* and the vernacular, *dhimotikí.* While there are somewhat different historical reasons for each, and while the functional distribution is somewhat different, they share a set of distinctions. In each case, the standard (or H, from Higher) variety is used for literacy and literary purposes and for formal, public, and official uses, while the vernacular (or L, from Lower) for informal conversation and daily use. Paralleling the differences in use are differences in form. The grammar of the L variety is generally simpler. For instance, fewer distinctions in the L variety are marked by the use of grammatical suffixes. There are also major differences in the vocabulary of the two varieties.

One of the major differences is understandably in the prestige of the two varieties. The H language is associated generally with a body of important literature and carries with it the prestige of a great tradition or religion. It is more stable, being protected from change by its association with written texts and by an educational system. It is also likely to be used over a wider region and thus can serve some unifying purpose. The L varieties are more localized and show dialectal variation and the tendency to change of unwritten dialects.

While developed originally to apply to cases of two varieties of the same language, the notion of diglossia can also be applied to the way in which two (or more) distinct languages come to divide up the domains in the linguistic repertoire of a speech community. In colonial situations, for instance, the language of the government takes on many of the attributes of an H language, while the various vernaculars fit the definition of an L language. For Navajo Indians, English fills the H function and Navajo the L. Another classic case is Paraguay, where Spanish is the H variety (used in literacy, education, and government, and associated with city life) and Guarani is the vernacular, spoken in the villages and used in the cities as a mark of informality and Paraguayan identity.

Diglossia thus refers to a society that has divided up its domains into two distinct clusters, using linguistic differences to demarcate the boundaries, and offering two clear identities to the members of the community. It is important also to note the political situations in which diglossia often occurs, with the H language associated with power. Educational pressure is normally in the direction of the H variety, and those who cannot master it are usually socially marginalized. At the same time, the L variety maintains value as a marker of membership of a peer or ethnic group.

While the classical diglossic cases have been stable for a long time, sociopolitical changes are starting to have their influence. Reference has been made to the possible emergence of an intermediate variety of Arabic, a kind of Educated Standard Arabic. In many countries, too, the globalization of English has introduced a third significant language, so that triglossia or polyglossia is starting to emerge. This tendency confirms our central theme, the close intertwining of social and linguistic structure, so that changes in one are reflected in changes in the other.

7
Applied sociolinguistics

Language policy and language planning

The very centrality of language to social life, the value of language as a means of access to power and influence, and the symbolic value of language in establishing social class and ethnic identity, all produce conditions where people want to engineer language or language choice itself.

In this chapter, we will look at a number of kinds of language planning or policy activities. These terms represent fashion rather than other differences. When sociolinguists started to be involved in the 1950s and 1960s, they preferred the term **language planning** as the term for any effort to modify language form or use. In the late 1980s, the regular failure of national planning activities seems to have encouraged the more neutral-seeming term, **language policy**.

Exactly where these activities arise depends in large measure on the perceived language situation of the social organization involved. For instance, in a situation where there are seen to be two or more languages available, any attempt to set up norms or rules for when to use each is what is called **status planning**. A decision to make one language official, or to ban another from use in school, or to conduct church services in a third, are cases of status planning. The most studied cases are in deciding on official or national languages for a newly independent state.

Once a language has been fixed as appropriate for use in a specific situation (i.e. as the official language, or in printing books, or in schools), any effort to fix or modify its structure is called **corpus planning**. The coining of new terminology for languages coping with modernization, or the Young Turk policy to remove Arabic words from Turkish, or the French efforts to rid the language of English words, or the Dutch decisions to change spelling, are all cases of corpus planning.

One aspect of corpus planning is the process of **language standardization**, which consists of attempting to standardize grammar and pronunciation towards some norm that is discovered or invented by some officially appointed or self-proclaimed group of language guardians. This process may be called **normativism** or prescriptivism by linguists who study it, or 'keeping the language pure' by those who carry it out.

A language status decision often produces a situation where some people need to learn a language that they do not normally speak. In Finland, for instance, the decision to recognize both Finnish and Swedish as official languages means that Finns must learn Swedish and Swedes Finnish. Sometimes called **language acquisition planning**, this process of **language education policy** is also involved when a government decides which foreign languages are to be taught in school or through other means. Similarly, a national policy to develop literacy in a language might be considered a kind of language acquisition policy.

For various reasons, a country or other social group may wish to encourage other people to learn their language. **Language diffusion policy** is sometimes associated with religious missionary work, as Islam spread Arabic, or with the national concerns of imperialist powers, as in Soviet activities to spread Russian throughout the USSR and Soviet-dominated Eastern Europe, or the French policy to spread *la francophonie*.

In countries where there is clear recognition of the existence of two or more respected languages and associated ethnic groups, such as Belgium, Switzerland, or Canada, status planning is an important activity. This is also the case in newly independent states where there exists a myriad of languages that must be chosen between, as in post-colonial India, Indonesia, or Nigeria. In a country where there is believed to be only one important language, and where other indigenous languages tend to be marginalized, the principal activity tends to be some aspect of corpus planning, such as the purification of the standard language.

Status planning

Status planning typically becomes an important activity when a country becomes independent, but it has probably already been a central concern of the nationalistic activities that preceded the actual independence. As mentioned earlier, nineteenth- and twentieth-century nationalist movements generally included a choice of a national language in their ideological package. Thus, newly independent Norway proclaimed its freedom in moving away from Danish power and language influence, but became involved in a bitter and continuing struggle as to what form of language to use; its eventual compromise has been to recognize the official equality of two varieties, called Riksmål and Nynorsk. The Irish nationalist movement took the restoration of Irish as its goal. The Zionist movement at the turn of the century proclaimed its interest not just in peoplehood and territorial regeneration, but in the restoration of Hebrew as a national language.

The decision is particularly harsh in a post-colonial state with a selection to be made among a number of indigenous language. In India, the costly and still uncertain solution was to recognize seven languages in the constitution. In many new African states, with the lack of congruence between language boundaries and the political borders that had been drawn as the colonialist powers carved up the continent, the choice among competing ethnic and tribal languages was part of a struggle for central power.

In these cases, the decision has often fallen on the colonial language as the official language for the new state. This is especially likely to be true in those cases where colonial policy was most successful in imposing belief in the value of the metropolitan language, and where the colonial language is only spoken, perhaps imperfectly, by a small educated elite. Such a policy was followed by France in all its territories and by Portugal in its colonies.

Issues concerning status planning continue to make headlines. New Zealand has finally agreed that the Treaty of Waitangi by which it obtained sovereignty over the Maori in 1840 requires it to recognize Maori as an official language alongside English. Post-apartheid South Africa ponders a language policy that will provide appropriate status alongside Afrikaans and English for the many languages spoken by the African majority, recalling no doubt that it was a language issue—riots in Soweto by African school children who were upset by a government decision to have them learn in Afrikaans rather than English—that may be considered the beginning of the successful campaign to destroy apartheid.

Language-status policy is by its very nature a political activity. Linguists are sometimes consulted, but decisions are made by government or elected parliament and sometimes form part of the constitution. The status decision determines which language or languages are to be used in various public functions, by government, the legal system, the media, and the educational system.

Sometimes there is an explicit policy spelled out by constitution or law. As mentioned earlier, the Indian constitution lists the seven constitutional languages and lays down their use for official and educational purposes. A recent French law (ruled unconstitutional by the constitutional court) attempted to make it illegal for public meetings (including international scientific congresses) to use languages other than French. The Soviet Constitution proclaimed that all languages were equal. The Quebec government passed a law requiring that all public signs and advertisements should appear only in French, and another that laid down that any child whose parents had not themselves gone to an English-language school in the province must have French-medium instruction.

In other cases, questions of language status are determined by national, regional, or local law, or are left to local practice. Present United States policy is a mixture of some local laws, some court-inspired recognition of language rights (see earlier discussion), and various local practices. Recently, however, a political campaign has begun to make English the only official language. In Israel, while Hebrew and Arabic are formally recognized as official languages for certain purposes, there is *de facto* recognition that most public signs are in English as well.

While the term 'official language' suggests governmental recognition, it is worth determining what precisely this status implies. In Quebec, the official status of French determines language use in signs and in education. In New Zealand, the official status of Maori effects mainly a requirement that government bodies adopt a Maori translation for their name and include it in their otherwise English announcements. In the respective Spanish autonomous regions, the new official status of Basque and Catalan involves a wider range of activities, including support for major government agencies concerned with the diffusion of the language. In the United States, the Voting Rights Act required the use in electoral ballots of major minority languages. In the constitution of the State of New Mexico written after its incorporation into the USA, there was a requirement for pharmacists to be bilingual in Spanish and English. In countries with recognition of the need for second language knowledge, there is often a requirement or a salary supplement for officials with the favoured competence.

Religious bodies often have significant language status policies. The decision of the Roman Catholic Church to change the language of the Mass from Latin to the local vernacular echoed a decision made four centuries earlier in the Reformation by the Protestant Churches. Hinduism, Orthodox Judaism, Islam, and Greek and Russian Orthodox Christianity, on the other hand, all have language policies which support maintenance of the status of a sacred language.

A political decision on the status of a language, if it is in fact to be implemented, usually leads to other activities. Often, a language whose status has changed needs to be modified in some way. This is corpus planning. And often it will need to be taught to people who do not speak it: this involves various kinds of language-diffusion policy, language-acquisition planning, or language-education policy.

Corpus planning

When it has been determined that the status of language is to be moved to a more elaborate level of standardization or to an expanded set of functions, the task of corpus planning begins. One of the most common processes is the need for modernization and elaboration of vocabulary. The rapid increase of concepts associated with the modern world, and the expansion of terminology needed to label all the new objects involved in modern technology, set a major challenge for all languages.

One obvious example is the *computer* I am working at now, which is a *laptop* or, to be more precise, a *sub-notebook*. I just had to have a new *motherboard* put in, as the old one would not accept the *PCMCIA card* that is supposed to be used to connect my *diskette drive*. But my *double-spaced hard drive* offers me a *megabyte* of *memory* (not to mention the 16-K *RAM* that my *programs* can access) and my *trackball* or *mouse* makes it easy to control my *passive matrix* screen. Most of the words I have italicized are ones that were not needed in English a decade ago, or have taken on new meanings quite recently. The problem facing any language that wishes to deal with the modern world is that it must keep up with the new developments.

There are some obvious choices. A language can simply take an old word (like *drive* or *screen*) and give it a new meaning. A *computer* in the Oxford English Dictionary (1933 edition) is a *person* who does calculations. A *mouse* still seems a quaint word to most of us for a pointing device. To say that a computer has a *memory* as a storage device is a pretty obvious metaphor (and, so I suspect, is *storage device*).

Another technique is to coin a new term, like *trackball*, *diskette*, or *megabyte*, by combining existing words or morphemes into more or less transparent forms. For many languages, the simplest technique would seem to be borrowing from another language where the term is in use because the concept or object has already been invented.

English is one language that has borrowed freely. From its beginnings in regular contact with first Danish, then French, its lexicon was constantly being enriched not just by coinages but by borrowing. During the periods of scientific and technological development, English freely coined new words based on Latin or Greek (or even, to the horror of Classical purists, with elements of both).

As part of his policy of unifying France, Cardinal Richelieu encouraged the establishment of the *Académie Française*, one of whose principal charges was to be to maintain the unity and purity of the French language. This it still continues to do, protesting regularly the tendency towards *Franglais* and the use of words like *le weekend* and *le biftek*.

One of the earliest kinds of corpus planning, called for as a language takes on official, standard, and educational functions as a result of changed status, is the developing of an **orthography**. Writing has not been invented very often, but more commonly it has been borrowed and adopted from one language to another. Most recent orthographies are slight modifications of other alphabets. The roman alphabet is most commonly used, under the influence of European languages. The Stalinist policy of linguistic centralization involved also changing the orthographies of many languages in the Soviet area of influence from Roman or Arabic orthography to the Cyrillic in which Russian and related languages are written. A major component of the Turkish Westernization movement was to change from Arabic to Roman script. Romanization has been proposed for Hebrew and Chinese, but with no success, for the weight of tradition has been too strong. The cost of maintaining a non-Roman alphabet is not small, as those who tried to develop a typewriter for them discovered, but computers are simplifying things.

But to develop an orthography is only a first step in the process of standardization and modernization; later, we will look at the related task of developing mass literacy.

Normativism and prescriptivism

When in 1970 a programme was started to teach Navajo children to read their own language, one of the first inconveniences was the absence of a typewriter that could produce the special diacritics and letters (a French acute accent, a Czech cedilla, and a Polish slashed Ł) that the developers of the Navajo orthography chose. (Incidentally, one of the few corpus planning decisions the Navajo Tribal Council made was to spell the name of the tribe in English with a 'j' rather than an 'h'.) A new problem soon turned up.

The first reading book one of the assistants wrote was a story of a cat, for which the writer used the Navajo word *mósi*. A little later, another writer included a cat in a book, but chose rather to write it *mási*. The Navajo dictionary, which had been written some thirty years before, listed both spellings. The Navajo linguist who had collaborated in writing the dictionary and was now a lecturer in the language at the Navajo Community College backed the dictionary, saying that he always told his students to write words as they and their family pronounced them. The spelling *mási* was therefore used in the second book, with a note for teachers in the back of the book that some people used *mási*, while others said *mósi*. The teachers were unhappy with this decision. They had been trained in English where there is usually only one correct spelling, and considered it wrong to be called on to teach rules that allowed too many choices.

In this attitude, they reflect the point of view of most Western-educated people who assume and expect that language rules are set, clear, unambiguous, and to be enforced. Some teachers of English as a foreign language complain in the same way about differences between British and American usage. This idea of 'correctness' is a mark of developed literate societies. In pre-literate societies, one regularly finds notions of 'a good speaker', by which is meant someone who has power to speak persuasively in public, but seldom the notion of 'correct' speech and spelling.

If you look at an Elizabethan book, you will note that printers were not concerned about 'correct' spelling, varying the spelling of the same word on a single line if it made the words fit in better. As printing and education spread, however, the notion of correctness became increasingly important. In the absence of an Academy legally charged with the task, dictionary and grammar-book writers took it upon themselves to describe and define what they considered standard and correct usage, and to prescribe these standards as required. Even when the description was clearly labelled as an arbitrary choice of one out of a number of varieties, it was generally accepted in a society seeking methods of gate-keeping as the mark of education and acceptability. George Bernard Shaw's *Pygmalion* (or the musical adaptation, *My Fair Lady*) is a touching and accurate account of how changes in speech and dress permitted a Cockney flower-girl to move into the high society from which she was otherwise barred.

Prescriptivism, therefore, is an understandable development in a mass education system where successful learning of prestige speech styles is a first step in social upward mobility. It is, however, unfortunately accompanied by a mistaken belief that speakers of non-standard varieties of a language are less intelligent, or less inherently capable than standard speakers. When linguists argue that all languages are equally good, they are attempting to fight the common prejudices that assume that standard languages and their speakers are inherently superior to non-standard languages and their speakers. Every variety, they maintain, has the potential to handle all tasks, and there is no evidence that people who speak a non-standard language are intellectually inferior to people who speak a standard language. At the same time, the normal association of the standard language with literacy and with formal education means that a key goal of many systems is to provide access to the standard language to the largest possible section of the population.

Language acquisition planning or language education policy

Teaching the standard language to all is one of the first tasks of most educational systems. In traditional religious education, the task of the religious school is usually to develop literacy in the language of the sacred texts: Hebrew for Jews, Classical Arabic for Moslems, Sanskrit for Hindus, Old Church Slavonic for Russian Orthodox, Giiz for Ethiopian Christians and Jews. In secular education, the equivalent first task is developing control of the written standard language.

The task is regularly complicated by the fact that the spoken language of the home is commonly not the standard written language of the school. In the case of languages of religious texts, this was usually obvious. Teachers in ultra-orthodox Jewish religious schools find it natural to teach Yiddish-speaking children in Yiddish to read texts written in Hebrew. In diglossic situations like those mentioned earlier, the problem is made more difficult, for the teachers and pupils sometimes have no respect for the L variety they actually speak, and claim or pretend to be speaking the H variety.

The first task of a formal educational system is usually, therefore, the teaching of the national standard language, with emphasis on literacy in it. Depending on social and political pressures, the system aims at students acquiring other varieties too. Especially in countries which recognize more than one language as part of the national tradition, there may be a programme to teach the other official language or languages. As noted earlier, for example, in Finland, all Finnish speakers are expected to learn Swedish and all Swedish speakers to learn Finnish. Similarly, in Quebec, all English speakers learn French and all French speakers learn English, and in Israel, Arab children learn Hebrew, and Arabic is in turn compulsory for Hebrew speakers.

Language diffusion policy or linguistic imperialism

Political and military conquest have been major causes of language spread. Aramaic in the ancient world, Greek in the Eastern Mediterranean, Latin in Western Europe, Arabic in the Middle East and North Africa, Mayan in Central America, Manding in West Africa are all cases. In these cases, the rulers did not follow an explicit policy of requiring the conquered to learn their languages, but essentially left the choice open. Similarly, when a language has been spread by trade (as for instance Swahili in Africa), the diffusion has been more or less unplanned. Even languages spread by missionary activity have not necessarily been the result of direct planning, for missionary groups commonly accept that the sacred texts will need to be translated if they are to be understood. It is for this reason that missionary activity so often leads to the development of vernacular literacy.

It is important to distinguish between this kind of unplanned language intervention, where altered circumstances encourage conquered or converted or commercialized populations to learn the language of their conquerors, missionaries and traders, from a planned **language diffusion policy**. In the first, we are dealing with the kinds of language shift we have talked about earlier; in the second we have a deliberate policy of a government or other institution to change language acquisition and use.

Language diffusion policy may be external or internal. When a country decides that all its inhabitants, whatever their home language, should learn and use the national language, we have a case of internal diffusion. When New Zealand started teaching all its Maori pupils in English in 1870; when the British required English in Welsh schools; when France would not allow Occitan, Breton, or Basque in its schools; when Stalin pushed for the use and higher status of Russian in all Soviet schools; or when China assumes that all pupils speak and should learn *Putonghoa*, these are all examples of language education policy that involve conscious and planned internal diffusion of a standard or official language.

Policy in conquered lands or colonies is both internal and external diffusion. Because the territory concerned is now under the control of the imperial rulers, it is not unnatural that they want to make governing easier by encouraging some, at least, of the colonial subjects to learn their language. Colonial language education policies have varied in their commitment to language diffusion. There have been, and continue to be, policies of language diffusion beyond national and even imperial boundaries. One of the earliest and strongest of these has been a French tradition of encouraging the spread of the French language beyond its national and colonial borders.

More recently, Germany has taken up language diffusion activities in its support for the Goethe Institute. A number of other countries work through the cultural attachés in their embassies or through semi-governmental bodies to encourage the diffusion of their national languages. Teaching the national language, as well as teaching about the national culture, is sometimes seen as an effective way of spreading influence and developing international interest in trade and tourism.

The spread of English—imperialism or hegemony?

The recent world-wide diffusion of English, so that it now looks set to become a world language, has raised not just concern among speakers of other languages, but controversy among sociolinguists. To what extent, they argue, is it the result of conscious planning by the governments and experts of English-speaking countries like the United Kingdom, the United States, Canada, South Africa, and Australia, and to what extent is it the result of a large array of factors connected with modernization and globalization?

A closer look at the process by which English has in this century developed into a global language suggests that in fact the demand has continually exceeded the supply. Language diffusion efforts of English-speaking countries have tended to be attempts to exploit world-wide desires to learn the language. There has been little need to fan the interest. The association of English with modern technology, with economic progress, and with internationalization, has encouraged people all over the world to learn English and to have their children learn it as early as possible. The more this has succeeded, the greater the reason for others to want to have access to the power and success assumed to be a result of knowing English.

The demand is not new: as early as the 1920s, Japanese and Chinese business leaders were starting to value knowledge of English. And it is deeply entrenched: even at the height of the Cultural Revolution in China, when there was deep suspicion of modernity and foreign influences, Chairman Mao continued to speak in favour of teaching English.

From the point of view of many observers, this growing linguistic hegemony of English is dangerous and harmful, and it is not unnatural to seek someone to blame. But whatever the cause, the spread of English is producing a new sociolinguistic reality, by threatening to take over important functions from other major languages, and by furthering language shift. It is an important task of sociolinguistics to understand this process.

Conclusions

Living languages are always changing, as they respond to changes in social structure. Language reflects society; it also serves to pass on social structure, for learning a language is a central feature of being socialized. Sociolinguistics is thus the study of language as it is used and of society as it communicates.

Because it is deeply concerned with language in society, sociolinguistics has from its start been equally involved in social matters. It is no wonder, therefore, that sociolinguists have had to come to grips with issues of social inequality, linguistically encoded and enforced discrimination, and the banning of languages, and the punishing of those who speak them. Hard as many sociolinguists try to describe dispassionately and scientifically what they see, they are regularly entangled in the efforts of minority groups to resist forced assimilation, or in defending speakers of stigmatized varieties from being considered ineducable. It is this regular ability to help that provides an extra incentive for so many sociolinguists

Less satisfying, perhaps, has been the failure to formulate any agreed central theory, so that the field seems to grow more complex all the time. While the various parts of the field are working with increasing precision to develop models that enable them to explain and predict sociolinguistic behaviour within the area of interest, no over-arching model or unified theory has been established to encourage the development of any single paradigm. One result is the freedom the sociolinguist has to explore new areas of interrelationship between language and society, and to continue to use increased understanding of the structure of one of the components to understand the other.

The central question remains the close intertwining between a language and the social context in which it is used. Language and society may not be purely human but they are such fundamental human phenomena that they cry out for better understanding.

SECTION 2
Readings

Chapter 1
The social study of language

Text 1

RONALD WARDHAUGH: *An Introduction to Sociolinguistics*
(2nd edn.) Blackwell 1992, pages 10–11

Sociolinguists are interested in the relationships between language and society. If we start off by defining 'society' as an organized group of people and 'language' as the way they communicate with each other, we have already set up one relationship between the two concepts. A society speaks a language. But there are other, more complex, relationships that might result. In the following passage, Ronald Wardhaugh suggests four possible relationships between the two.

There is a variety of possible relationships between language and society. One is that social structure may either influence or determine linguistic structure and/or behaviour. Certain evidence may be adduced to support this view: the *age-grading* phenomenon, whereby young children speak differently from older children and, in turn, children speak differently from mature adults; studies which show that the varieties of language that speakers use reflect such matters as their regional, social, or ethnic origin and possibly even their sex; and other studies which show that particular ways of speaking, choices of words, and even rules for conversing are determined by certain social requirements. We will also find that 'power' is a useful concept that will help explain much linguistic behaviour. Power, as both something to achieve and something to resist, exerts considerable influence on the language choices that many people make.

A second possible relationship is directly opposed to the first: linguistic structure and/or behaviour may either influence or determine social structure. This is the view that is behind the Whorfian hypothesis, the claims of Bernstein, and many of those who argue that languages rather than speakers of these languages can be 'sexist'. A third possible relationship is that the influence is bi-directional: language and society may influence each other. One variant of this approach is that this influence is dialectical in nature, a Marxian view put forward by Dittmar, who argues that 'speech behaviour and social behaviour are in a state of constant interaction' and that 'material living conditions' are an important factor in the relationship.

A fourth possibility is to assume that there is no relationship *at all* between linguistic structure and social structure and that each is independent of the other. A variant of this possibility would be to say that, although there might be some such relationship, present attempts to characterize it are essentially premature, given what we know about both language and society.

▷ *What evidence does the writer mention for the effects of social structure on language?*

▷ *In many languages, one uses the masculine pronoun to refer to either a male or a female (for example, 'Every student should hand in his work in time.') Is this 'sexist'? Can you think of other cases?*

▷ *What evidence could you give for and against the 'no relationship' position?*

Text 2

JAMES MILROY: *Linguistic Variation and Change.* Blackwell 1992, pages 5–6

Presumably, the best way to observe the relationship between language and society is when language is being used in a social situation. For this reason, Milroy argues that we should first look at language being used in a conversation.

Speech is a social activity in a sense that writing is not, and the primary locus of speech is *conversation*. Conversations take place between two or more participants in social and situational contexts, and linguistic change is one type of phenomenon that is passed from person to person in these situations. The first principle for a socially based model of language change therefore concerns the *observation* of language in use: it is the principle that speech exchanges can be observed only within social and situational contexts—they can never be devoid of such a context. To express this more fully:

> *Principle I*
> As language use (outside of literary modes and laboratory experiments) cannot take place *except* in social and situational contexts and, when observed, is *always* observed in these contexts, our analysis—if it is to be adequate—*must* take account of society, situation and the speaker/listener.

This first principle carries with it a number of implications, the most important of which is that generalizations about language structure depend on a process of abstracting 'language' from the situational contexts in which it naturally occurs. We do not actually observe 'the language' or 'language' in the abstract: we observe people talking. In a social account of language change, therefore, we have to explain how changes get into this abstract structure that we call language (which we cannot observe directly) as a result of the activities of people talking (which we can observe more directly). Furthermore, unstructured observations of very selective phenomena will not be enough here: our descriptions of sociolinguistic patterns will depend on observing recurrent patterns and will have to be systematic and accountable to the data. . . . It also follows from this first principle that close attention to methods of data collection and analysis (and the relation of one to the other) is crucial. . . .

Whereas Principle I concerns the impossibility of *observing language* independently of society, Principle 2 concerns the impossibility of *describing* language structures independently of society. This is not as controversial as it may seem.

> *Principle 2*
> A full description of the structure of a variety (whether it is

'standard' English, or a dialect, or a style or register) can only be successfully made if quite substantial decisions, or judgements, of a social kind are taken into account in the description.

The word 'social' here does not mean social class or prestige—the decisions (or judgements) we are talking about are decisions (or judgements) about the 'norms' of the variety concerned, and these norms are social in the sense that they are *agreed on* socially—they depend on consensus among speakers within the community or communities concerned and will differ from one community to another.

▷ *'Speech is a social activity in a sense that writing is not.' In what sense?*

▷ *What kinds of observation, according to the writer, are needed in order to obtain reliable information about language variation?*

▷ *Why does the description of the structure of a society depend on 'judgements of a social kind'?*

Text 3

WILLIAM LABOV: *The Social Stratification of English in New York City*. Center for Applied Linguistics 1996, pages 91–2

If we accept the argument that our primary data should come from language in social use, the question remains of how to collect it. The problem is that the observer (the data collector) adds another party to the conversation.

For accurate information on speech behavior, we will eventually need to compare the performance of large numbers of speakers. Furthermore, we will want to study a sample which is representative of a much larger group, and possibly of the New York speech community as a whole. This cannot be done without random sampling. Yet to complete random sampling, and to make the data for many speakers comparable, we need structured, formal interviews. Here is the paradox which we sensed: the formal interview itself defines a speech context in which only one speaking style normally occurs, what we may call CAREFUL SPEECH.

The bulk of the informant's speech production at other times may be quite different. He may use careful speech in many other contexts, but on most occasions he will be paying much less attention to his own speech, and employ a more relaxed style which we may call CASUAL SPEECH. We can hear this casual speech on the streets of New York, in bars, on the subway, at the beach, or whenever we visit friends in the city. Yet anonymous observations in these contexts will also be biased. Our friends are a very special group, and so too are those New Yorkers who frequent bars, play stickball in the streets, visit public beaches, or talk loud enough in restaurants to be overheard. Only through a painstaking method of sampling the entire population, and interviewing speakers chosen at random, can we avoid serious bias in our presentation. The problem is now to see what can be accomplished within the bounds of the interview.

▷ *Why are structured, formal interviews needed?*

▷ *How does the presence of a stranger with a recording instrument define the situational context?*

▷ *How would this interfere with observing casual speech?*

▷ *Why will anonymous observation in public places also produce a biased picture?*

Text 4

JOSHUA A. FISHMAN: 'The sociology of language' in Joshua A. Fishman (ed.): *Advances in the Sociology of Language*. Mouton 1971, Vol. 1, page 221

One of the important contributions of sociolinguists to the study of language has been the effort to determine the social value that is accorded to any variety. The writer argues that it is not just the existence of difference that is important, but the 'symbolic value' given to a language or variety that determines whether people use it or not. Just as different kinds of clothing can keep us equally warm, but a uniform symbolizes the group we belong to, so different varieties also come to carry value as symbols of group membership.

All in all, the sociology of language seeks to discover not only the societal rules or norms that explain and constrain language behaviour and *the behaviour toward language* in speech communities but it also seeks to determine the symbolic value of language for their speakers. That language varieties come to have symbolic symptomatic value, in and of themselves, is an inevitable consequence of their functional differentiation. If certain varieties are indicative of certain interests, of certain backgrounds, or of certain origins, then they come to represent the ties and aspirations, the limitations and the opportunities with which these interests, backgrounds and origins, in turn, are associated. Language varieties rise and fall in symbolic value as the status of their most characteristic or marked functions rises and falls. Varieties come to represent intimacy and equality if they are most typically learned and employed in interactions that stress such bonds between interlocutors. Other varieties come to represent educated status or national identification as a result of the attainments associated with their use and their users and as a result of their realisation in situations and relationships that pertain to formal learning or to particular ideologies. However, these functions are capable of change.... The step-by-step elevation of most modern European vernaculars to their current positions as languages of culture and technology is only one example of how dramatically the operative and symbolic functions of languages can change. Similar changes are ongoing today.

▷ *Many people argue that all kinds of language are 'equal', by which they mean presumably that they are equally useful. How does Fishman's idea of symbolic value challenge this idea?*

▷ *What kind of symbolic value does a national language carry with it? Does this help one understand how national movements pick a language?*

▷ *Thinking about ongoing changes, how does the symbolic value of languages set a problem for the European Community or for any other multilingual community?*

Chapter 2
The ethnography of speaking and the structure of conversation

Text 5

RALPH FASOLD: *The Sociolinguistics of Language.*
Blackwell 1990, pages 40–1

Just as languages can vary, there can be fundamental differences from one community to another in the rules of how language is used. There can be different rules about when to speak and when to be silent.

To understand what the ethnography of communication is all about, it is necessary to understand some fundamental concepts. It is one of Hymes's emphases that ways of speaking can vary substantially from one culture to another, even in the most fundamental ways. For example, it has been pointed out (for instance, Schegloff 1972) that most middle-class white Americans (and possibly members of other Western societies as well) have a 'no gap, no overlap' rule for conversational turn-taking. If two or more people are engaged in conversation and if two speakers start to talk at the same time, one will very quickly yield to the other, so that the speech of two people does not 'overlap'. On the other hand, if there is a lull in the conversation of more than a few seconds' duration, the participants become extremely uncomfortable. Someone will start talking about something unimportant just to fill the 'gap' or the group will break up.

So profoundly ingrained is this rule for speakers who have it that they can hardly imagine a conversation being carried on in any other way. But Reisman (1974) found that it was quite the usual practice for Antiguans to carry on discussions with more than one speaker speaking simultaneously. On the other hand, Saville-Troike (1982) reports that there are American Indian groups where it is common for a person to wait several minutes in silence before answering a question or taking a speaking turn. Reisman (1974: 112) tells [a] story about his experiences in a Lapp community in northern Sweden, where conversational gaps are part of the ordinary way people talk. ...

Obviously, an ethnography of communication for middle-class

white Americans would include the 'no gap, no overlap' conversational rule. The corresponding description of Antiguan speech rules would not include the 'no overlap' rule. And a description of the American Indian groups Saville-Troike refers to, or the Lapps that Reisman lived near, would not include the 'no gap' rule.

▷ *How would people in your community react to Antiguan speech style, or to the American Indian speech style that Saville-Troike talks about?*

▷ *Do you have the 'no gap' or the 'no overlap' rule in your speech community? How do people interpret breaches of the rule?*

Text 6

PENELOPE BROWN: 'How and why are women more polite: some evidence from a Mayan community' in Sally McConnell-Ginet, Ruth Borker, and Nelly Furman (eds.): *Women and Language in Literature and Society*. Praeger 1980, pages 114–15

Most speakers are aware that in certain situations, when talking to certain people, they need to take special care of their speech. Being polite, Brown argues, is taking care not to hurt other people. But, she goes on, there is more than one way of being polite.

What politeness essentially consists in is a special way of treating people, saying and doing things, in such a way as to take into account the other person's feelings. On the whole that means that what one says politely will be less straightforward or more complicated than what one would say if one wasn't taking the other's feelings into account.

Two aspects of people's feelings seem to be involved. One arises when whatever one is now about to say may be unwelcome: the addressee may not want to hear that bit of news, or be reminded of that fact, or be asked to cooperate in that endeavor. A request, for example, or anything that requires a definite response directly imposes on the addressee. One way of being polite in such situations is to apologize for the imposition and to make it easy for the addressee to refuse to comply. So we try to give the most interactional leeway possible, and this, in one sense, is what it is to be polite.

Our long-term relations with people can also be important in taking their feelings into account. To maintain an ongoing relationship with others, one greets them on meeting in the street, inquires about their health and their family, expresses interest in their current goings-on and appreciation of the things they do and like and want.

These two ways of showing consideration for people's feelings can be related to a single notion: that of FACE. Two aspects of people's feelings enter into face: desires to not be imposed upon (negative face), and desires to be liked, admired, ratified, related to positively (positive face). Both can be subsumed in the one notion of face because it seems that both are involved in the folk notion of 'face loss.' If I walk past my neighbor on the street and pointedly fail to greet him, I offend his face; and if I barge into his house and demand to borrow his lawnmower with no hesitation or apology for intrusion (for example, 'Give me your lawnmower; I want it') I equally offend his face. So blatantly and without apologies *imposing on* and blatantly and without apologies *ignoring* the people with whom one has social relationships are two basic ways of offending their faces. Three factors seem to be involved in deciding whether or not to take the trouble to be polite:

1 One tends to be more polite to people who are socially superior to oneself, or socially important: one's boss, the vicar, the doctor, the president.

2 One also tends to be more polite to people one doesn't know, people who are somehow socially distant: strangers, persons from very different walks of life.

In the first situation politeness tends to go one way upwards (the superior is not so polite to an inferior), while in the second situation politeness tends to be symmetrically exchanged by both parties.

3 A third factor is that kinds of acts in a society come ranked as more or less imposing, and hence more or less face threatening,

and the more face threatening, the more polite one is likely to be.

These three factors appear to be the main determinants of the overall level of politeness a speaker will use.

▷ *Think of some examples of what Brown calls negative face, and some of positive face. Then consider how they should be ranked. Is this ranking likely to be universal?*

▷ *How is politeness related to social structure?*

▷ *In what social conditions do you think that women are likely to be more polite than men?*

Text 7

ELAINE CHAIKA: *Language: The Social Mirror* (2nd edn.) Newbury House 1989, page 44

Another area of language, the structure of which is easily observed, is greetings. Here, too, we try to be polite. Like the ringing of the telephone, greetings serve to start conversations. But, like other kinds of politeness, they set the tone and help establish the relationship between the speakers.

Greetings have two functions. One is to initiate interaction; the other, which will concern us first, is what cultural anthropologist Bronislaw Malinowski (1923) called phatic communication, speech not to convey thoughts but to create 'ties of union ... by mere exchange of words.' Phatic communication is speech for the sake of social contact, speech used much the way we pat dogs on the head as a way of letting them know we care.

Greeting, even if in passing, is essential to let members of society know that they count, and that 'everything is all right.' Most often, this is to indicate that there are no hard feelings or anger on the part of the greeter, although, in the event of a cold greeting, it may indicate that there are still hard feelings. If acquaintances fail to say 'Hi' when we know that they have seen us, we feel hurt. Such a trivial omission, yet we give it a name, a snub. We are obliged to greet even when we cannot or do not want to get into a conversation. For this reason, perhaps, the person greeted is supposed just to acknowledge the greeting phatically, not launch into a recital of 'what's happenin'' or even the ills of the day. The response 'Fine' can properly end the greeting sequence. Whether or not the person is truly fine is immaterial. Phatic communication has been completed with its utterance. If the greeter wants to know more, such as why 'fine' was uttered glumly, he or she can stop and ask for more information. At this juncture, it is proper to go into details. Greeting, therefore, fulfills two functions: first, the requirements of phatic communication, and second (if desired on the part of the greeter), opening further interaction.

▷ *What is wrong with giving details in answer to a greeting 'How are you?'*

▷ *Under what circumstances is it considered appropriate behaviour not to greet someone?*

▷ *How many different forms of greeting do you use? Can you explain the circumstances under which you use them?*

Chapter 3
Locating variation in speech

Text 8
JOHN GUMPERZ: 'The speech community' in David L. Sills (ed.): *International Encyclopedia of the Social Sciences.* Macmillan 1968, Vol. 9

The writer argues for the double function of language, both communicating information by referring to extralinguistic reality, and communicating social information about the users. The system operates in what Gumperz defines as a speech community, for which he proposes a linguistic definition.

Although not all communication is linguistic, language is by far the most powerful and versatile medium of communication; all known human groups possess language. Unlike other sign systems, the verbal system can, through the minute refinement of its grammatical and semantic structure, be made to refer to a wide variety of objects and concepts. At the same time, verbal interaction is a social process in which utterances are selected in accordance with socially recognized norms and expectations. It follows that linguistic phenomena are analysable both within the context of language itself and within the broader context of social behavior. In the formal analysis of language the object of attention is a particular body of linguistic data abstracted from the settings in which it occurs and studied primarily from the point of view of its referential function. In analysing linguistic phenomena within a socially defined universe, however, the study is of language usage as it reflects more general behavior norms. This universe is the speech community: any human aggregate characterized by regular and frequent interaction by means of a shared body of verbal signs and set off from similar aggregates by significant differences in language usage.

Most groups of any permanence, be they small bands bounded by face-to-face contact, modern nations divisible into smaller subregions, or even occupational associations or neighborhood gangs, may be treated as speech communities, provided they show linguistic peculiarities that warrant special study. The verbal behavior of such groups always constitutes a system. It must be based on finite sets of grammatical rules that underlie the production of well-formed sentences, or else messages will not be intelligible.

▷ *What kinds of communication are there besides linguistic communication?*

▷ *Does Gumperz allow for multilingual and non-geographical speech communities?*

▷ *Does this definition set any size for a speech community?*

▷ *Do any non-linguistic features enter into Gumperz' definition of a speech community?*

Text 9

GLYN WILLIAMS: *Sociolinguistics: A Sociological Critique.* Routledge 1992, page 72

The writer of this next piece disagrees with Gumperz for his over-reliance on linguistic criteria. In the rest of the book, he challenges other sociolinguists for their failure to take into full account theories in sociology.

One feature which the concept of speech community shares with the sociological concept of community is interaction. This much is evident in the quotation from Gumperz's work cited above. It encompasses a view of things reminiscent of the social dialectology of the nineteenth century with the emphasis on boundaries determined by language which in turn is determined by social factors. The important features of Gumperz's definition are interaction and language use although we should not disregard his reference to verbal signs. The concept once again appears to be the product of linguistic rather than social factors since the boundaries are defined by linguistic features. However, it would be a sterile concept if it was discussed simply in terms of linguistic uniformity. Thus we have the possibility of 'differences' in language use which relate to interactional factors. The attributes of difference which serve to define the speech community are linguistic rather than social and they have the result of producing 'aggregates' rather than social groups in the sociological sense. Thus, it would appear that the speech community is an aggregate of individuals in interaction.

▷ *What does the writer think that Gumperz' definition of speech community has in common with the sociological idea of community?*

▷ *In what way is a speech community defined by 'interaction and language use' different from dialect 'boundaries defined by language features'?*

▷ *What is 'sterile' about the idea of 'linguistic uniformity'?*

Text 10
J.K CHAMBERS and PETER TRUDGILL: *Dialectology.*
Cambridge University Press 1980, page 5

How does one distinguish between a language and dialect? Not just on linguistic grounds. Nor is it simple to distinguish between a dialect and an accent, although generally we use 'accent' to mean a difference in pronunciation.

It seems, then, that while the criterion of mutual intelligibility may have some relevance, it is not especially useful in helping us to decide what is and is not a language. In fact, our discussion of the Scandinavian languages and German suggests that (unless we want to change radically our everyday assumptions about what a language is) we have to recognise that, paradoxically enough, a 'language' is not a particularly linguistic notion at all. Linguistic features obviously come into it, but it is clear that we consider Norwegian, Swedish, Danish and German to be single languages for reasons that are as much political, geographical, historical, sociological and cultural as linguistic. It is of course relevant that all three Scandinavian languages have distinct, codified, standardised forms, with their own orthographies, grammar books, and literatures; that they correspond to three separate nation states; and that their speakers consider that they speak different languages.

The term 'language' is thus from a linguistic point of view a relatively non-technical term. If therefore we wish to be more rigorous in our use of descriptive labels we have to employ other terminology. One we shall be using in this book is VARIETY. We shall use 'variety' as a neutral term to apply to any particular kind of language which we wish, for some purpose, to consider as a single entity. The term will be used in ad hoc manner in order to be as specific as we wish for a particular purpose. We can, for example, refer to the variety 'Yorkshire English', but we can equally well refer to 'Leeds English' as a variety, or 'middle class Leeds English'—and so on. More particular terms will be ACCENT and DIALECT. 'Accent' refers to the way in which a speaker pronounces, therefore refers to a variety which is phonetically and/or phonologically different from other varieties. 'Dialect', on the other hand, refers to varieties which are grammatically (and perhaps lexically) as well as phonologically different from other varieties. If two speakers say, respectively, *I done it last night* and *I did it last night*, we can say that are speaking different dialects.

▷ *Two languages or dialects or other varieties are 'mutually intelligible' when a person who speaks one can understand a person speaking the other. Are there dialects of English or your own language that you cannot understand?*

▷ *What makes Danish and Norwegian separate languages?*

▷ *What does it mean to say that 'variety' is a 'neutral' term?*

▷ *What would it suggest if you were told someone speaks American English with a British accent?*

Chapter 4
Styles, gender, and social class

Text 11
GREGORY R. GUY: 'Language and social class' in Frederick J. Newmeyer (ed.): *Linguistics: The Cambridge Survey.* Cambridge University Press 1988, Vol. IV, page 37

One obvious effect of social structure on language should be that groups that are divided socially should also show linguistic differences. Three obvious kinds of social division are by gender, by age-grading (as mentioned in Text 1 above), and by social class.

In all human societies individuals will differ from one another in the way they speak. Some of these differences are idiosyncratic, but others are systematically associated with particular groups of people. The most obvious of these are associated with sex and developmental level: women speak differently from men, and children differently from adults. These two dimensions of social variation in language are in part biologically determined (for example, differences in laryngeal size producing different pitch levels for adult men and women), but in most societies they go beyond this to become conventional and socially symbolic. Thus men and women differ by far more in language use than mere pitch. (In fact, even their pitch differences are more pronounced than can be anatomically explained.) Such sociosymbolic aspects of language use serve an emblematic function: they identify the speaker as belonging to a particular group, or having a particular social identity.

In many societies some of the most important of these sociolinguistic divisions are associated with differences in social prestige, wealth, and power. Bankers clearly do not talk the same as bus-boys, and professors don't sound like plumbers. They signal the social differences between them by features of their phonology, grammar, and lexical choice, just as they do extralinguistically by their choices in clothing, cars, and so on. The social groups at issue here may be harder to define than groups like 'men' and 'women,' but they are just as real. They are the divisions of a society along lines of SOCIAL CLASS.

Class divisions are essentially based on status and power in a society. Status refers to whether people are respected and deferred to by others in their society (or, conversely, looked down on or ignored), and power refers to the social and material resources a person can command, the ability (and social right) to make decisions and influence events.

▷ *What does the writer think are the most obvious systematic differences in people that lead to differences in the way they speak? How might these differences be biological or innate?*

▷ *How do differences in speech show group membership?*

▷ *Do you agree that the choice of phonology, grammar, and lexicon is like the choice of clothing or a car? If not, how is it different?*

▷ *Might the language differences associated with gender and age be equally well explained as the result of differences in status and power?*

Text 12

EDMUND A. AUNGER: 'Regional, national and official languages in Belgium' in *International Journal of the Sociology of Language* 104, 1993, pages 44–5

Belgium recognizes three languages, Dutch, French, and German, and classifies all the languages people speak in the home and the neighbourhood as dialects.

The great majority of Belgians speak an indigenous, but largely unstandardized, regional language: West Flemish, Brabantish, Limburgish, Luxemburgish, Walloon, Picard, Lorrain, or Champenois. These are Belgium's private tongues, the languages of family, friends, and neighbors. Use of these languages is primarily oral, rather than written. Although standardized spelling systems are often available, these are not widely used by the language communities. The Belgian State has effectively refused to recognize these languages by classifying them as dialects of

Dutch, German, or French. This policy, characterized more by neglect than by outright repression, has contributed to the decline of the regional languages. There have been occasional, but belated, exceptions to this pattern. Walloon, Picard, and Lorrain may now be taught in the French language schools—by virtue of a 1982 decision of the Executive of the French Community—but, in fact, very few schools have ever offered courses in these languages. In a neighboring state, the Grand Duchy of Luxembourg, Luxemburgish is recognized as the national language, and it is the language of instruction for the first year of elementary school.

Belgium's linguistic identity has been shaped by its recognition of three standardized languages—French, Dutch, and German—as national languages. This recognition, dating from 1866, has had a profound effect on the choice of official languages. After decades of protracted debate, the Belgian State has recognized French, Dutch, and, to a limited extent, German as its official languages. French and Dutch are the languages of the Belgian parliament, and all laws have been published in these two languages since 1898. Public employees in the central administration are listed on a French roll or a Dutch roll, and all government positions are classed by language. Justice is conducted in the language of the region, and judges must be proficient in that language. Similarly, school instruction is in the language of the region—French, Dutch, or German. These, therefore, are Belgium's public tongues, the languages of political power and public affairs.

▷ *What eleven languages does the writer claim to be spoken in Belgium?*

▷ *Would the writer agree with the definition of language and dialect suggested in Text 10 above?*

▷ *What are the legal consequences of the recognition of the three official languages?*

Text 13

JANET HOLMES: *An Introduction to Sociolinguistics.*
Longman 1992, pages 171–2

Among other differences between the speech of men and women, one that has been the source of considerable debate is the fact that women tend to use more standard forms of language than do men with the same educational level.

Some linguists have suggested that women use more standard speech forms than men because they are more status-conscious than men. The claim is that women are more aware of the fact that the way they speak signals their social class background or social status in the community. Standard speech forms are generally associated with high social status, and so, according to this explanation, women use more standard speech forms as a way of claiming such status. It is suggested that this is especially true for women who do not have paid employment, since they cannot use their occupations as a basis for signalling social status.

The fact that women interviewed in New York and in Norwich reported that they used more standard forms than they actually did, has also been used to support this explanation. Women generally lack status in the society, and so, it is suggested, some try to acquire it by using standard speech forms, and by reporting that they use even more of these forms than they actually do.

Though it sounds superficially plausible, there is at least some indirect evidence which throws doubt on this explanation. It is suggested that women who are not in paid employment are most likely to claim high social status by using more standard forms. This implies that women in the paid workforce should use fewer standard forms than women working in the home. But the little evidence that we have, in fact suggests that just the opposite may be true. An American study compared the speech of women in service occupations, working in garages and hotels, for instance, with the speech of women working in the home. Those in paid employment used more standard forms than those working in the home. In the course of their jobs, the first group of women were interacting with people who used more standard forms, and this interaction had its effect on their own usage. By contrast, the women who stayed home interacted mainly with each other, and this reinforced their preference for vernacular forms.

Exactly the same pattern was found in an Irish working-class community. The younger women in Ballymacarrett, a suburb of Belfast, found work outside the community, and used a much higher percentage of linguistic features associated with high status groups than the older women who were working at home. This evidence thus throws some doubt on suggestions that women without paid employment are more likely to use standard forms than those with jobs, and so indirectly questions the social status explanation for women's speech patterns.

▷ *Do you think that any of the suggested explanations have anything to do with biological differences between men and women?*

▷ *Why might sociolinguists think that women are more status-conscious than men?*

▷ *Why did the American women working in garages and hotels use more standard forms than those who stayed home?*

Chapter 5
Bilinguals and bilingualism

Text 14
GEORGE SAUNDERS: *Bilingual Children: Guidance for the Family*. Multilingual Matters Ltd 1983, page 9

For some people, a bilingual is a person with equal control of two languages, for others, it is someone with full control of one and limited control of a second. Given this uncertainty, the issue of classification is important.

How proficient does a person have to be, then, to be classed as a bilingual? Haugen, an American linguist who has worked extensively in the field of bilingualism, suggests that bilingualism begins 'at the point where a speaker of one language can produce complete, meaningful utterances in the other language'. Diebold considers that a type of bilingualism has even commenced when a person begins to *understand* utterances in a second language without being able to utter anything him- or herself.

Bilingualism, therefore, simply means having two languages (and bilingualism is often used in the literature to mean the same as multilingualism, that is, having more than two languages). Bilinguals can be ranged along a continuum from the rare equilingual who is indistinguishable from a native speaker in both languages at one end to the person who has just begun to acquire a second language at the other end. They are all bilinguals, but possessing different *degrees* of bilingualism. A monolingual (also called a unilingual or monoglot) is thus someone who knows only one language. (In this book monolingual is used, for the sake of convenience, to refer also to persons near the extremity of the bilingualism continuum, namely to persons who are minimally bilingual, that is, who have very little proficiency in more than one language.)

A bilingual's degree of bilingualism can be assessed in the four skills of listening comprehension, speaking, reading comprehension and writing. There are many possible combinations of abilities in these skills. Many children of immigrants, for instance, possess all four skills solely in the official language of their country of residence (for example, English in Australia), whilst they may be able to understand only the spoken form of their parents' language (for example, Italian) and barely be able to speak it. Haas would class such children as 'receiving oral bilinguals', since they are bilingual only in receiving the spoken form of two languages, in listening comprehension. Someone who is bilingual in all four skills would, using this system, be classified as a 'receiving sending oral visual bilingual'. Again, within each skill there could be differing abilities in each language, for example, an English Chinese bilingual educated through English could be much more proficient at writing English than Chinese, whereas his spoken Chinese could be better than his spoken English, and so on.

The term 'balanced bilingual' is frequently encountered in the literature on bilingualism. Whilst some writers (for example, Haugen) use it as a synonym of equilingual, most researchers use 'balanced bilingualism' in a different sense which does not imply perfect mastery of both languages (for example, Peal & Lambert). Balanced bilinguals in this sense are bilinguals who are roughly equally skilled in their two languages, i.e. a balance exists between the two.

▷ *Would any of these definitions consider some who has learned a foreign language at school a bilingual? Is it useful to do so?*

▷ *How might you determine if someone is bilingual?*

> *How might someone become a 'balanced bilingual'? How common is this likely to be?*

Text 15

CAROL MYERS-SCOTTON: *Social Motivations for Codeswitching: Evidence from Africa*. Clarendon Press 1993, pages 1–2

The mixing of two languages is often seen as the result of laziness, and as the cause of weakening of a language. Codeswitching is very common among bilinguals, and Myers-Scotton suggests that it serves important social functions.

Everyday conversations in two languages are the subject-matter of this volume. All over the world bilinguals carry on such conversations, from Hispanics in Texas, who may alternate between Spanish and English in informal in-group conversations, to West Africans, who may use both Wolof and French in the same conversation on the streets of Dakar, Senegal, to residents in the Swiss capital of Berne, who may change back and forth between Swiss German and French in a service exchange. Contrary to some popular beliefs, such conversations are not mainly a transitional stage in a language shift from dominance in one language to another. It is true that many immigrants who are in the process of language shift do engage in codeswitching, but this form of conversation is also part of the daily lives of many 'stable' bilingual populations as well. Neither is codeswitching only the vehicle of social groups on the socioeconomic 'margins' of society; for example, in every nation, successful business people and professionals who happen to have a different home language from the language dominant in the society where they live frequently engage in codeswitching (between these two languages) with friends and business associates who share their linguistic repertoires. Consider Punjabi-origin physicians in Birmingham, England, Lebanese-origin businessmen in Dearborn, Michigan, or Chinese-origin corporate executives in Singapore.

Codeswitching is the term used to identify alternations of linguistic varieties within the same conversation. While some prefer to discuss such alternation under two terms, employing *code-mixing* as well as *codeswitching*, the single term *codeswitching* is used here. ... The linguistic varieties participating in codeswitching may be different languages, or dialects or styles of the same language.

▷ *Where is codeswitching most likely to occur? What happens if a bilingual codeswitches when talking to a monolingual?*

▷ *How might codeswitching account for all the Norman French words that are now part of English?*

Chapter 6
Societal multilingualism

Text 16
F. NIYI AKINNASO: 'Vernacular literacy in modern Nigeria' in *International Journal of the Sociology of Language* 119, 1996, pages 46–7

When a country has a very large number of languages spoken in it, each comes to fill a different role in the national linguistic repertoire

Nigeria's complicated sociolinguistic landscape reveals three major types of languages: (1) about 400 indigenous languages; (2) three exogenous languages—Arabic, English, and French; and (3) a relatively 'neutral' language, namely, Pidgin English. The languages form a hierarchy, characterized by a 'six language-formula,' in which the languages are stratified according to the degree of official recognition, prestige, range and context of use, extent of development, population of speakers, and so forth. ... The most outstanding feature of Nigeria's language-planning model, therefore, is the adoption of a system of stratified rationalization in which one or more majority languages are accorded some special status at federal, regional, state, and local levels, while the right of other languages to exist and be developed is also respected. This favorable attitude to language rights underlies the language education policy and, especially, the attitude toward the development of local languages and their use in literacy.

English is clearly at the top of the language hierarchy, carrying the heaviest functional load as the language of much of administration, education, mass communication, commerce, and judicial proceedings in the higher courts. Besides being the language of literate professions (law, medicine, engineering, accountancy, etc.) as well as the nation's library and archival language, English is also a medium of interethnic and international communication. In keeping with its colonial legacy, it remains as the nation's *de facto* 'official' language, being the language of the constitution and of legislation *(Constitution of the Federal Republic of Nigeria [henceforth Constitution]* 1989, Section 53). English, therefore, carries the highest symbolic value. ... As the language of mainstream institutions and activities, it is the most desirable language that parents want their children to learn in school. ...

The four hundred or so indigenous languages occupy various positions below English, with three—Hausa, Igbo, and Yoruba—being officially recognized as 'major' languages, to be learned in school in addition to the mother tongue and English, and accorded (at least in principle) almost equal status with English in that they are recognized in the constitution as legislative languages, to be so used 'when adequate arrangements have been made therefor' *(Constitution,* Section 53). The three languages are also used in the communications media for network news broadcasts on radio and television, for newspaper publication, and for environmental print (billboards, notices, graffiti, etc.). ... Of all Nigerian languages, these three are the most developed and have the longest history of involvement in literacy use in and outside the mainstream.

▷ *Why does English have the highest status in Nigeria?*

▷ *What indigenous languages share some of this status?*

▷ *What languages are used in the media, and why do you think this is so?*

▷ *What language is used for communication between ethnic groups?*

▷ *How is the notion of language status related to the notion of symbolic value (see Text 4)?*

Text 17

PETER MÜHLHÄUSLER: *Pidgin and Creole Linguistics.*
Blackwell 1986, pages 84–5

Pidgins start off filling important but limited roles as lingue franche (the plural of lingua franca) or languages of wider communication, but often develop a growing range of functions and increasing complexity.

Continued use of a stable pidgin by speakers from many different language backgrounds, particularly when transported from the plantation to a larger multilingual society such as that of Papua New Guinea or Vanuatu, led to further functional and structural expansion. On the one hand, the permanency of contacts required the encoding of personal feelings; on the other, social norms of politeness such as small talk were needed. The addition of the expressive function typically goes hand in hand with a widening of domain. In many instances, the use of a pidgin for religious purposes triggered this new functional use. Phatic communion (a term introduced by Malinowski 1923) is associated with new domains (meetings, social gatherings, etc.) as well as new media. In using a pidgin for telephone conversations, for instance, certain devices referring to this channel of communication and its functioning are required.

It has to be kept in mind, at all times, that pidgins are second languages and that any new functions have to be seen in relation to the functional use of a speaker's first language. The use of a jargon—that is, a language for propositional and heuristic functions only—typically has little effect on a speaker's vernacular. It is simply added to it. The same is true with beginning stabilizing pidgins and many older stable pidgins: they are additional to traditional vernaculars, which continue to remain intact and to be used in all functions relevant to the traditional society in which they are spoken.

With the ongoing functional and structural expansion of a pidgin, however, its relationship with the speaker's first language tends to become changed. Instead of being added to, traditional languages tend to be replaced in an increasing number of domains and functions. This is particularly striking with the expressive function in the domains of religion and abuse. Thus the religious experiences transmitted by expatriate mission bodies to the indigenous population tend to be incompatible with traditional modes of religious expression and pidgins, or mission lingue franche are preferred. Prayer, services and discussion of religious matters thus are associated with speakers' second languages. The same is true of insults, expletives and other forms of strong language. For Tok Pisin among the Kwoma, Reed observed:

> We found that youngsters not only counted and sang in pidgin but also used it in the new game of football—especially in angry altercations. Their own language was not lacking in terms of abuse, but those in pidgin were preferred. (Reed 1943: 286)

▷ *What led to the greater demands on pidgins?*

▷ *What additional functions might a new channel make?*

▷ *What is expressive about religion and abuse?*

Text 18

PETER TRUDGILL: *On Dialect: Social and Geographical Perspectives.* Blackwell 1983, page 127

You can't be an X unless you speak Xish. Replace X by the name of an ethnic group and Xish by the name of the associated language, and you have a statement with which many will agree. But Trudgill points out that the situation is more complex.

It is well known that language can act as an important defining characteristic of ethnic group membership, and in many communities the link between language and ethnicity is strong, and obvious. It also has to be recognized, however, that a simple equation of ethnic and language group membership is far from adequate. There are, obviously, many examples of situations where a separate ethnic identity is maintained even though a distinctive language has been lost (see Fishman, 1968). Examples include the British Jewish community, and the Catholic community in Northern Ireland. (In some cases of this sort, dialect or accent differences within a single language may serve as identifying characteristics—Trudgill, 1974b, chapter 3.) More puzzling, perhaps, are cases where language distinctiveness appears not to be accompanied by any awareness of a separate ethnic identity. To what extent, for example, do Gaelic-speaking Scots form a separate ethnic group within Scotland?

It is not easy to determine what factors are involved in the establishment of these varying attitudes to language and ethnic group membership.

▷ *Can you think of other exceptional cases where ethnic groups are distinct despite language similarity, or where language differences do not mark ethnic differences?*

▷ *What do you think are the other defining features of an ethnic group besides language?*

Text 19

PETER LADEFOGED: 'Another view of endangered languages' in *Language* 68/4, 1992, pages 810–11

In a paper published in early 1992, Ken Hale and a number of colleagues, all of them active in the study of American Indian languages, drew attention to the fact that a large number of the 6000 or so languages still being spoken are in serious danger of disappearing in the next 100 years or less. They took the position that linguists should help preserve these endangered languages. Peter Ladefoged expresses a somewhat different view.

So now let me challenge directly the assumption of these papers that different languages, and even different cultures, always ought to be preserved. It is paternalistic of linguists to assume that they know what is best for the community. One can be a responsible linguist and yet regard the loss of a particular language, or even a whole group of languages, as far from a 'catastrophic destruction' (Hale et al. 1992: 7). Statements such as 'just as the extinction of any animal species diminishes our world, so does the extinction of any language' (Hale et al. 1992: 8) are appeals to our emotions, not to our reason. The case for studying endangered languages is very strong on linguistic grounds. It is often enormously strong on humanitarian grounds as well. But it would be self-serving of linguists to pretend that this is always the case. We must be wary of arguments based on political considerations. Of course I am no more in favor of genocide or repression of minorities than I am of people dying of tuberculosis or starving through ignorance. We should always be sensitive to the concerns of the people whose language we are studying. But we should not assume that we know what is best for them.

We may also note that human societies are not like animal species. The world is remarkably resilient in the preservation of diversity; different cultures are always dying while new ones arise. They may not be based on ethnicity or language, but the differences remain. Societies will always produce subgroups as varied as computer nerds, valley girls, and drug pushers, who think and behave in different ways. In the popular view the world is becoming more homogeneous, but that may be because we are not seeing the new difference that are arising. Consider two groups of Bushmen, the Zhuloãsi and the !Xóõ who speak mutually unintelligible languages belonging to different subgroups of the Khoisan family, but otherwise behave in very similar ways. Are these two groups more culturally diverse than Appalachian coalminers, Iowa farmers and Beverly Hills lawyers? As a linguist, I am of course saddened by the vast amount of linguistic and cultural knowledge that is disappearing, and I am delighted that the National Science Foundation has sponsored our UCLA research, in which we try to record for posterity the phonetic structures of some of the languages that will not be around much longer. But it is not for me to assess the virtues of programs for language preservation versus those of competitive programs for tuberculosis eradication, which may also need government funds.

In this changing world, the task of the linguist is to lay out the facts concerning a given linguistic situation. ...

Last summer I was working on Dahalo, a rapidly dying Cushitic language, spoken by a few hundred people in a rural district of Kenya. I asked one of our consultants whether his teen-aged sons spoke Dahalo. 'No,' he said. 'They can still hear it, but they cannot speak it. They speak only Swahili.' He was smiling when he said it, and did not seem to regret it. He was proud that his sons had been to school, and knew things that he did not. Who am I to say that he was wrong?

▷ What attitude does the writer take to language decline?

▷ What reasons does the writer cite for studying endangered languages? Does he think that these reasons are equally valid?

▷ Would you advise a speaker of Dahalo to teach the language to his or her children? Why?

Chapter 7
Applied sociolinguistics

Text 20

E. GLYN LEWIS: 'Movements and agencies of language spread: Wales and the Soviet Union compared' in Robert L. Cooper (ed.): *Language Spread: Studies in Diffusion and Language Change*. Indiana University Press 1982, pages 231–2

Colonization and immigration are among the most important causes of language change. But these are not simple forces, as the following analysis suggests.

The present linguistic and ethnic composition of the populations of Britain (so far as concerns the Celtic countries) and the Soviet Union is in each case the product of the conquest of some territories, the more or less pacific acquisition of others, colonization, and massive immigration—all acting on primordially native groups and interacting with each other. The United States and Canada, on the one hand, the Soviet Union and the Celtic-speaking peoples of Britain, on the other, exemplify two different but complementary processes of colonization and immigration. So far as North America is concerned, where very many different peoples have been attracted to one continent from many parts of the world—an intensive process of ethnic and linguistic *convergence*—the colonial movement is *centripetal*. In the case of Britain (English) and the USSR (Russian) the process has been *centrifugal*. English diffused in order to assimilate the peripheral Celtic lands to the north and west of Britain, as well as North America, while Russian from its Kievan and Muscovite bases spread to the European west and sought out the diverse Asian nations of the south and east. To all intents the United States, in spite of the predominance of the English language, has been a nation of *induced* diversity. Diversity was an inescapable consequence whatever attempts were made to ignore it; so that the American problem has always been to ensure unity while accommodating diversity. On the other hand, Russia and now the Soviet Union has always set out to *acquire* diversity. It was always able to enforce Russian political unity and prepare for linguistic dominance by its military strength and by the cult of the Orthodox Church, and now by the promotion of a single party, a uniform ideology. From its point of view the problem has been to acknowledge (without sustaining) the inescapable linguistic diversity within a uniform political system. Britain attempted to suppress linguistic diversity, and the Soviet Union began by seeking to preserve it. The different processes of colonization have resulted in different emphases on aspects of the intractable problem of the relation of linguistic unity and diversity, which is at the root of language spread.

▷ *What is the difference between a centripetal and a centrifugal language policy?*

▷ *Why does the writer consider the problem of the relations of linguistic unity and diversity to be intractable? Do you know of anywhere that it has been solved?*

▷ *In the new independent countries like Ukraine and Estonia there are now strong movements for establishing the dominance of the national language over Russian. Would this development have surprised Lewis?*

Text 21

ROBERT L. COOPER: *Language Planning and Language Change.* Cambridge University Press 1989, pages 118–19

While the notion of active policies to change the status of languages is not new, the study of language planning started with the problems of newly independent states in the post-Second World War period, many of which had to choose between a number of indigenous languages and one or more colonial languages. Canada is one country where, more than two hundred years after the political situation was established that brought French and English into conflict, tension continues to surround language status.

Perhaps the best-known example of status planning for work is found in the Province of Quebec, which from the mid-1970s has sought to make French rather than English the language of work. Although Francophones comprise about 80 percent of the population, control of economic and financial institutions is concentrated in the hands of the Anglophone minority and foreign Anglophones. Although Francophones have entered middle management in large numbers, Anglophones are overwhelmingly dominant at the top managerial level of large business firms. Francophone workers who aim to enter the ranks of top management have felt obliged to learn English. Material incentives to learn English have inspired non-Anglophone, non-Francophone immigrants (termed 'Allophones') to learn English rather than French and to identify themselves with the Anglophones rather than with the Francophone community. The position of French has been further undermined by a falling birth rate among Francophones, who increasingly have felt their relative importance in the Province to be threatened. Accordingly, even before the Quebec nationalist Parti Québécois came to power in 1976, the province adopted legislation to promote French as the language of work.

In 1974, the Liberal Party's Bill 22, the 'Official Languages Act,' which made French the official language of Quebec, also declared that business personnel must be able to communicate in French, and compelled private businesses to develop a 'francization program,' leading to the use of French at all levels of employment, in order to receive certain government benefits and to compete for government contracts. In 1977, the provincial government, under the Parti Québécois, adopted Bill 101, the 'Charter of the French Language,' which broadened the scope of these provisions. The charter stipulated that all businesses employing at least fifty persons must obtain a certificate stating either that the firm is applying a francization program or that no such program is needed (Daoust-Blais 1983). The Charter established a mechanism for implementing these provisions, including coercive measures to ensure compliance. Bill 22 and Bill 101 provide an unusually clear recognition of the importance of commercial incentives for the promotion and defense of language maintenance. They also provide clear recognition that status planning refers ultimately to the status of those who use the language.

▷ *What was the status of French before Bill 22 and Bill 101?*

▷ *What was the goal of Bill 22?*

▷ *How did Bill 101 strengthen this?*

▷ *What conflict does this show between the symbolic value (see Text 4) and the usefulness of a language?*

Text 22

CALVIN VELTMAN: 'The English language in Quebec 1940–1990' in Joshua A. Fishman, Alma Rubal-Lopez, and Andrew W. Conrad (eds.): *Post-Imperial English: Status Changes in Former British and American Colonies, 1940–1900*. Mouton de Gruyter 1996, pages 232–3

Summing up the effect of the language status planning under-taken in Quebec (see Text 21), Veltman looks at the situation more than a decade after the two Bills were enacted.

The demographic situation of the English-speaking group has also undergone marked changes, changes which make it difficult to imagine that the trends which we have examined in this chapter can be reversed or even arrested. First of all, the French language group is now attracting about two immigrants in every three among third language groups, leaving the English language group with substantially fewer new recruits than in the past. This has already had a marked effect on the English language school system and will undoubtedly reduce the clientele of all the institutions of the English-speaking community in the future.

Second, there has been a substantial reduction in the number of English-speaking immigrants from the United States, the United Kingdom, and from English Canada itself over the past thirty years. Quebec is no longer seen as a preferential destination for English-speaking immigrants. Further, recent data suggest that at least 10 percent of anglophone immigrants from outside Canada during the decade of the 1980s have integrated into the French language community, testimony indeed to the new attractive power of the French language.

In addition, it would seem likely that the trend toward greater francisation of the workplace will continue. While the English language schools have made pioneering attempts to teach French to their children, the segregated character of Quebec's institutional structure and of many residential neighborhoods makes it difficult for anglophone children to learn French well enough to be comfortable in the workplace. Consequently, the pressure to emigrate in order to capitalize on their educational achievements will not likely abate. Studies continue to show that many young anglophones, including those who reportedly speak French well, indicate that they too will leave Quebec when they finish their education. Not only will this process deprive the English language group of its potential leadership; it deprives the school system and the community in general of the next generation of children.

In short, while English-speaking people in Quebec continue to enjoy a greater range of privileges, rights, and services than do French language minorities in English Canada, the transition from a dominant group to a minority group has been an extremely painful one. English-speaking people can still be served in English in almost all situations of daily life; most anglophones continue to live in relatively segregated environments where French is hardly, if ever, spoken. Although they can obtain government services of all types in English and their children can go to English schools, colleges, and universities, the official status accorded English is not sufficient to dispel the sentiment that the presence of English-speaking people is not as much appreciated as it should be. Unable to escape from the pressures to learn and speak French well, particularly in the workplace, many English-speaking people view migration to an English-speaking society as an important option. This choice has been the principal cause of the decline of the English-speaking group, and it is likely to presage significant decline in the future.

▷ *What was the effect of the Bills on the English-speaking population of Quebec?*

▷ *Did the Bills lead to greater integration of the two populations?*

▷ *How does the Quebec example show the potential and limitations of political efforts to change a sociolinguistics situation?*

SECTION 3
References

The references which follow can be classified into introductory level (marked ■□□), more advanced and consequently more technical (marked ■■□), and specialized, very demanding (marked ■■■).

Chapter 1
The social study of language

■□□

RALPH FASOLD: *The Sociolinguistics of Language: Introduction to Sociolinguistics, II*. Blackwell 1990

Among a number of useful general introductory textbooks that now cover the field, this book stands out for its coverage of the effect of social class on patterns of language use.

■□□

JOSHUA A. FISHMAN: *Sociolinguistics: A Brief Introduction*. Newbury House Publishers 1970

Written as the field of sociolinguistics was taking shape, this short book by one of the leading theorists in the field summarizes the main concerns that are still debated. It is written clearly and introduces many basic concepts.

■■■

JOSHUA A. FISHMAN: 'Putting the "socio" back into the sociolinguistic enterprise' in *International Journal of the Sociology of Language* 92, 1991, pages 127–38

More than anyone else, Joshua Fishman has worried about the difficulties that the field has had in maintaining its relationships with one of its parent disciplines. This paper discusses the nature of the problem and argues for a closer relation with sociology.

■□□

JANET HOLMES: *An Introduction to Sociolinguistics*. Longman 1992

This is a another introductory textbook, with good general coverage and a strong section on language and gender.

■□□

RONALD WARDHAUGH: *An Introduction to Sociolinguistics* (2nd edn.) Blackwell 1992

This standard introduction to the field is now in its second edition. It covers the main issues clearly and soundly.

Chapter 2
The ethnography of speaking and the structure of conversation

■■■

ALAN BELL: 'Language style as audience design' in *Language in Society* 13/2, 1984, pages 145–204

The level of formality is generally considered a result of how much attention a speaker is paying to his or her speech. Basing his analysis first on radio announcers, Bell suggests that it can be better understood by considering the speaker's intended audience.

■■■

ERVING GOFFMAN: 'Replies and responses' in *Language in Society* 5/3, 1976, pages 257–313

This pioneering essay investigated the structure of telephone conversations and became the model for studies of conversational structure.

■■□

ALLEN D. GRIMSHAW (ed.): *Conflict Talk: Sociolinguistic Investigations of Arguments in Conversation.* Cambridge University Press 1990

This collection of papers shows how the field of conversational analysis has developed. It concentrates on disagreement.

■■□

JOHN J. GUMPERZ, ed.: *Languages and Social Identity.* Cambridge University Press 1982

This is a collection of papers that consider, from an ethnographic perspective, the way language is used to communicate a speaker's choice of identity.

■■□

DELL HYMES: *Foundations in Sociolinguistics: An Ethnographic Approach.* University of Pennsylvania Press 1974

This is an approach to sociolinguistics from the point of view of an anthropological linguist who proposed the key notion of communicative competence.

■■□

TAMAR KATRIEL: 'Brogez: Ritual and strategy in Israeli children's conflicts' in *Language in Society* 14/4, 1985, pages 467–90

This article is a good example of the way an ethnographer investigates the language use patterns of young children. It analyses the way that young Israeli children formalize conflicts and disagreements, and how they make peace after such fights.

Chapter 3
Locating variation in speech

■■□

J.K. CHAMBERS: *Dialectology*. Cambridge University Press
1980

A short and useful introduction to the field, this book summarizes
basic principles.

■■□

CHARLES A. FERGUSON: *Sociolinguistic Perspectives:
Papers on Language and Society*, 1959–1994.
Oxford University Press 1996

This is a collection of brilliant pioneering observations on the
nature of language in use by a scholar who has had great influence
on the development of sociolinguistics.

■■■

LESLEY MILROY: *Observing and Analyzing Natural
Language*. Blackwell 1987

This is a detailed study of the nature of social variation in language use and structure.

■□□

PETER TRUDGILL: *The Dialects of English*. Blackwell 1990

This general description of the dialects of English is written with
full appreciation of the relevance of sociolinguistics.

Chapter 4
Styles, gender, and social class

■■□

ROGER BROWN and ALBERT GILMAN: 'The pronouns of
power and solidarity' in Thomas A. Sebeok (ed.): *Style in
Language*. MIT Press 1960, pages 253–76

This is a pioneering study that started a whole series of investigations into systems of address.

■■□

BETTY LOU DUBOIS and ISABEL CROUCH: 'The question of tag questions in women's speech: they don't really use more of them, do they?' in *Language in Society* 4/3, 1975, pages 289–94

There are many stereotypes about the way that women use language. This is an empirical study of the use of tag questions that shows that often the stereotypes are wrong.

■□□

JANET HOLMES: *Women, Men and Politeness*. Longman 1995

Are men or women more polite? If so, why? This book investigates this key question about differences between women's and men's language.

■□□

ROBIN LAKOFF: 'Language and woman's place' in *Language in Society* 2/1, 1973, pages 45–80

This is a pioneering essay on women's language. While not all of its generalizations have held up, it was influential in opening a new field of study.

■■■

WILLIAM LABOV: *Sociolinguistic Patterns*. University of Pennsylvania Press 1972

This book, by one of the most important and influential scholars in the field, studies the relation between social and linguistic structure, showing how by adding social information one can account more fully for language variation.

■□□

DEBORAH TANNEN: *Gender and Discourse*. Oxford University Press 1996

This is a collection of essays on gender and language which provides a good picture of current concerns.

Chapter 5
Bilinguals and bilingualism

■■☐

CHARLOTTE HOFFMAN: *An Introduction to Bilingualism.*
Longman 1991

This book surveys the major issues concerning the nature of bilingualism and the studies that have been made of the phenomenon.

■■■

JOHN EDWARDS: 'Monolingualism, bilingualism and
identity: lessons and insights from recent Canadian
experience' in *Current Issues in Language and Society* 2/1,
1995, pages 5–38

Canada has been the location of many studies of bilingualism.
This article shows the way language choice intersects with social
and political identity.

■■☐

CHARLES A. FERGUSON: 'Diglossia' in *Word* 15, 1959,
pages 325–40

The phenomenon of two varieties of the same language with
separate sets of functions was first set out in this paper.

■■■

JOSHUA A. FISHMAN, ROBERT L. COOPER, and ROXANA
MA: *Bilingualism in the Barrio.* Research Center for the
Language Sciences, Indiana University 1971

A pioneering study of a stable bilingual community, this book had
a major impact on the development of the sociology of language,
its methods and theories. It is a detailed study of a urban bilingual
community, showing how an immigrant minority interacts with
its new environment.

■■■

CAROL MYERS-SCOTTON: *Social Motivations for
Codeswitching: Evidence from Africa.* Oxford Studies in
Language Contact, Clarendon Press 1993

This book present a theory of language choice, with extensive illustration from codeswitching in several African contexts.

Chapter 6
Societal multilingualism

■■□

E. GLYN LEWIS: *Multilingualism in the Soviet Union.* Mouton 1972

The former Soviet Union was marked by a complex pattern of multilingualism. This book describes it, and shows the changes in governmental attitude and policy through the Soviet period. It shows linguistic imperialism in an extreme form.

■■■

JOSHUA A. FISHMAN (ed.): *Advances in the Study of Societal Multilingualism.* Mouton 1978

This is a collection of papers dealing with multilingualism in various parts of the world.

■■■

EINAR HAUGEN: 'Language and immigration' in *Norwegian-American Studies and Records* 10, 1938, pages 1–43

This is a pioneering study of Norwegian in America showing the effects of immigration on patterns of language use.

■■□

JOSHUA A. FISHMAN: *Reversing Language Shift: Theoretical and Empirical Foundations of Assistance to Threatened Languages*, Multilingual Matters Ltd 1991

Social and demographic changes have led this century to the growth of major languages and a strong tendency for less powerful languages to be lost. This study looks at recent efforts by speakers of these endangered languages to resist language shift, and presents a theoretical model of how such resistance can work.

■■□

CHRISTINA BRATT PAULSTON (ed.): *International Handbook of Bilingualism and Bilingual Education.* Greenwood Press 1988

This volume includes descriptions of multilingualism and of the associated bilingual and multilingual educational patterns in a wide variety of countries.

■■□

BERNARD SPOLSKY and ROBERT L. COOPER: *The Languages of Jerusalem.* Clarendon Press 1991

This is a study of the history and current sociolinguistic pattern of a multilingual city.

Chapter 7
Applied sociolinguistics

■□□

COLIN BAKER: *Foundations of Bilingual Education and Bilingualism.* Multilingual Matters Ltd 1993

This book summarizes the possible educational responses to the existence of multilingual societies.

■■□

ROBERT L. COOPER: *Language Planning and Social Change.* Cambridge University Press 1989

This is a highly readable survey of the field of language planning and policy which sets out clearly the main issues in the field.

■■■

JOSHUA A FISHMAN, ALMA RUBAL-LOPEZ, and ANDREW W. CONRAD (eds.): *Post-Imperial English: Status Changes in Former British and American Colonies, 1940–1990.* Mouton de Gruyter 1996

This book includes a number of empirical studies of the spread of English in countries that were at one time British or American colonies. It provides a basis for answering the question of how and why English has spread.

■■□

FRED GENESEE: *Learning through Two Languages: Studies of Immersion and Bilingual Education*. Newbury House Publishers 1987

Including mainly empirical studies of bilingual education in Canada, this book investigates an educational policy in which speakers of one language start their education in another.

■■■

TINA HICKEY and JENNY WILLIAMS (eds.): *Language, Education and Society in a Changing World*. IRAAL/Multilingual Matters Ltd 1996

This is a collection of papers on various aspects of educational linguistics, showing current attempts to deal with multilingualism.

■■□

RICHARD D. LAMBERT (ed.): *Language Planning around the World: Contexts and Systematic Change*. National Foreign Language Center 1994

This book collects a number of articles dealing with language and language education policy in various parts of the world.

■■□

ROBERT PHILLIPSON: *Linguistic Imperialism*. Oxford University Press 1992

This book presents evidence and arguments in support of the case that the spread of English is largely the result of conscious planning on the part of those English-speaking countries that stand to gain by its international use.

■■■

TOVE SKUTNABB-KANGAS: *Bilingualism or Not: The Education of Minorities*. Trans. L. Malmberg and D. Crane. Multilingual Matters Ltd 1981

This book documents a large number of cases where educational and other policies have forced minorities to give up their own languages.

SECTION 4
Glossary

Page references to Section 1, Survey, are given at the end of each entry.

accommodation Adjusting one's speech to converge with or diverge from the speech of one's interlocutor. [33, 42]

anthropocentric speech Use of the masculine (man, he) to include the feminine. *See* **accommodation theory**. [38]

audience design Adjusting one's speech to be similar to that of a real or imagined listener. [33, 41]

baby talk A **register** regarded as appropriate for addressing babies. [44]

balanced bilingualism Very strong (almost equal) command of two languages. [45]

bilingual A person who has some functional ability in a second language. [45]

Black English The **vernacular** variety used by Afro-Americans in the US, sometimes called Ebonics or Afro-American Vernacular English. [63]

borrowing The integration of a word from one language into another. [49]

cant Thieves' and underworld **jargons**. [34]

clandestine recording Collecting data surreptitiously. [10]

code switching Changing from language to language in the midst of an utterance. [49]

competence Underlying knowledge of a language; cf. **performance**. [48]

compound bilinguals **Bilinguals** who learned one language after (and so through) another; cf. **co-ordinate bilinguals**. [48]

conversational interchange The basic unit of the spoken language, where two or more speakers take turns to speak. *See* **turn-taking**. [16]

co-ordinate bilinguals Bilinguals who have learned each language in separate contexts and so keep them distinct; cf. **compound bilinguals**. [48]

corpus planning An attempt to fix or modify the structure (writing system, spelling, grammar, vocabulary) of a language. [66]

creole A **pidgin** once it has native speakers. *See* **creolization**. [62]

creolization Changes in a **pidgin** as a result of adding **vitality** or mother tongue speakers. [62]

diachronic variation Changes in a language over time. *See* **historical linguistics**; cf. **synchronic variation**. [4]

dialect A **variety** of a language used recognizably in a specific region or (a social dialect) by a specific social class. [27]

dialectology The search for spatially and geographically determined differences in various aspects of language. [28]

diglossia A situation when two distinct **varieties** of the same language are used, side by side, for two different sets of functions. [63]

domain Typical social situation with three defining characteristics: place, role-relationship, and topic. [34]

endangered language Language that is no longer being passed on to children as a native language, but is spoken by a contracting and aging group of adults. *See* **language loss**. [55]

ethnographic observation The recording of natural speech events by a participant-observer. [12]

ethnography of speaking Sometimes also called the ethnography of communication, an anthropological approach to the study of language use which is based on the actual observation of speech. [14]

floor The right to talk at any given moment in a conversation. *See* **turn-taking**. [19]

formality Degree of care taken with speech. *See* **style**. [31]

free variation The notion that the choice of **variant** is uncontrolled and without significance. [39]

gender (1) A grammatical class; (2) a term for socially marked sexual variation. [36]

generic masculine Use of the grammatically masculine form (*man*, *he*) to include the feminine. *See* **anthropocentric speech**. [38]

genre Kind of **speech event**, or kind of literary form. [15]

historical linguistics The study of language change over time. *See* **diachronic variation**. [27]

hypercorrection Tendency to over-use socially desirable features in careful speech and reading. [41]

interference A feature of one language appearing when speaking or writing another. [49]

jargon Speech used by a marked group of people such as a trade or occupation; cf. **cant, slang**. [33]

language acquisition planning, or **language education policy** Policy determining which languages should be taught and learned. [67]

language conflict Situation where two or more languages compete for status. [55]

language contact Situation where two or more languages are brought into contact by virtue of **bilingualism**. [49, 55]

language diffusion policy Policy to spread a language to people who do not speak it. [67, 75]

language loss A process by which speakers of a language slowly stop using it, resulting in its dying out. *See* **endangered language**. [59]

language loyalty The ability (or lack of it) of speakers of a language to stand up to the pressure of more powerful ones. [55]

language maintenance A situation where speakers continue to use a language even when there is a new language available. [55]

language of wider communication Language chosen by speakers of several different languages to communicate with each other. [61]

language planning, or **language policy** Any effort to modify language form or use. [66]

language shift Changes in the degree of functional use from one language to another. [55]

language standardization The imposing of a norm on the grammar and pronunciation of a language. [67]

macrosociolinguistics or the **sociology of language** Area of sociolinguistic study which concentrates on the use of a variety and its social significance. [6]

metaphorical switching Changing from one language to another to signal a change in role relationship; cf. **code switching**. [50]

microsociolinguistics Area of sociolinguistic study which concentrates on linguistic variables and their significance. [6]

mixed code A variety with extensive code switching used by **bilinguals** to talk to each other. [49]

networks Groups of people who communicate with each other regularly. [26]

non-intrusive responses A research technique involving asking strangers short non-personal questions. [11]

normativism The claim that there is one 'correct' version and all variation is deviant. [33, 67]

observer's paradox How can we observe the way people speak when they are not being observed? [8]

orthography Writing (and spelling) system. [72]

performance Linguistic behaviour (as opposed to linguistic knowledge); cf. **competence**. [48]

pidgin A variety of language that is not a native language of anyone, but is learned in contact situations; cf. **creole**, **creolization**. [61]

politeness Recognition of other's rights in a social situation. [19]

post-creole continuum When speakers of a **creole** or **pidgin** are introduced, usually by education, to the standard language on which the creole or pidgin was originally based. [62]

register Variety associated with a specific function. [33]

repertoire Collection of varieties or languages spoken by a group of people. *See* **speech community**. [25]

reversing language shift Efforts by a group to resist **language loss**. [57]

revitalization The restoration to a language of **vitality**. [56]

service encounters Occasions in which one person (client, customer, patient) seeks help from another (seller, clerk). [17]

slang A kind of **jargon** marked by its rejection of formal rules. *See* **cant**. [35]

social stratification The study of class distinction in speech. [39]

sociolinguistic interview Technique of a recorded conversation intended to collect speech samples. [10]

sociology of language *See* **microsociolinguistics**. [6]

solidarity Feeling of shared experience and common group membership. [35]

speech community (1) All the people who speak a single language (like English or French or Amharic); (2) a complex interlocking network of communication whose members share knowledge about and attitudes towards language use. [24]

speech event Act of human communication. [14]

status planning Any attempt to set up laws or norms for when to use a language. [66]

stereotypes Fixed and prejudicial patterns of thought about kinds of people that are often mistaken. [28, 37]

styles Varieties of language used by an individual appropriate to a level of **formality**. [4, 31]

synchronic variation Variation at a single point of time; cf. **diachronic variation**. [4]

terms of address Second-person pronouns, or names, or titles, used when speaking to someone. [20]

turn-holders Ways of signalling that the speaker intends to continue after a break, intended to keep the **floor**. [19]

turn-taking Rules for determining who speaks when in a conversational interchange. *See* **floor**. [18]

variable A linguistic feature (a sound, word, or grammatical form) which has more than one **variant**, each of which has a sociolinguistic significance. [11]

variant A form (word, sound, or grammatical form) which alternates with another under definable conditions. *See* **variable.** [6, 11, 29]

variety A term used to denote any identifiable kind of language. [6]

vernacular A **variety** used in common or popular speech; not the educated or standard variety. [8]

vitality Natural intergenerational transmission (the language is learned as a mother tongue). [56]

Acknowledgements

The author and publisher are grateful to the following for permission to reproduce extracts from copyright material:

Addison Wesley Longman for an extract from Janet Holmes: *An Introduction to Sociolinguistics* (Longman 1992).

Blackwell Publishers for extracts from Ralph Fasold: *The Sociolinguistics of Language* (Blackwell 1990); James Milroy: *Linguistic Variation and Change: On the Historical Sociolinguistics of English* (1992); Peter Mühlhäusler: *Pidgin and Creole Linguistics* (1986); Peter Trudgill: *On Dialect: Social and Geographical Perspectives* (1983); and Ronald Wardhaugh: *An Introduction to Sociolinguistics*, 2nd edn. (1992).

Cambridge University Press for extracts from J. K. Chambers and Peter Trudgill: *Dialectology* (1980); Gregory R. Guy: 'Language and social class' in *Linguistics: The Cambridge Survey* edited by Frederick J. Newmayer (1988); and Robert L. Cooper: *Language Planning and Language Change* (1989).

Center for Applied Linguistics for extracts from William Labov: *The Social Stratification of English in New York City* (1966); and E. Glyn Lewis: 'Movements and agencies of language spread: Wales and the Soviet Union compared' in *Language Spread: Studies of Diffusion and Language Change* edited by Robert L. Cooper (Indiana University Press, 1982).

Greenwood Publishing Group, Inc. for an extract from Penelope Brown: 'How and why are women more polite: some evidence from a Mayan community' in *Women and Language in Literature and Society* edited by Sally McConnell-Ginet, Ruth Borker, and Nelly Furman (Praeger 1980).

Indiana University Press for an extract from E. Glyn Lewis: 'Movements and agencies of language spread: Wales and the Soviet Union compared' in *Language Spread: Studies of Diffusion and Language Change* edited by Robert L. Cooper (1982).

Linguistic Society of America for an extract from Peter Ladefoged: 'Another view of endangered languages' in *Language* 68 (1992).

Macmillan Library Reference USA, a Simon and Schuster Macmillan Company, for an extract from John J. Gumperz: 'Linguistics: the speech community' in *International Encyclopedia of the Social Sciences* edited by David L. Sills, Vol. 9, Copyright © 1968 by Crowell Collier and Macmillan, Inc. Copyright renewed © 1996.

Mouton de Gruyter, a division of Walter de Gruyter & Co, Publishers for extracts from F. Niyi Akinnaso: 'Vernacular literacy in modern Nigeria' in *International Journal of the Sociology of Language*, 119 (W. de Gruyter 1996); Edmund A. Aunger: 'Regional, national and official languages in Belgium' in *International Journal of the Sociology of Language*, 104 (W. de Gruyter 1993); Joshua A. Fishman: 'The sociology of language' in *Advances in the Sociology of Language* Vol. 1 edited by Joshua A. Fishman (Mouton 1971); and Calvin Veltman: ' The English language in Quebec 1940–1990' in *Post-Imperial English: Status Changes in Former British and American Colonies 1940–1990*, edited by Joshua A. Fishman *et al.* (Mouton 1996).

Multilingual Matters Ltd for an extract from George Sanders: *Bilingual Children: Guidance for the Family* (1983).

Oxford University Press for an extract from Carol Myers-Scotton: introduction to *Social Motivations for Codeswitching: Evidence from Africa* (Clarendon Press 1993).

Routledge for an extract from Glyn Williams: *Sociolinguistics: A Sociological Critique* (1992).

Despite every effort to trace and contact copyright holders before publication, there are cases where this has not been possible. If notified the publisher will be pleased to rectify any errors or omissions at the earliest opportunity.